OUT *of the* DEPTHS

JOHN NEWTON

Revised and Updated for Today's Readers
by Dennis R. Hillman

Kregel
Publications

Out of the Depths by John Newton
Revised and Updated for Today's Readers by
Dennis R. Hillman

© 2003 Kregel Publications

Published by Kregel Publications, a division of Kregel, Inc.,
P.O. Box 2607, Grand Rapids, MI 49501.

Image of John Newton in later life, used on the back cover,
courtesy of the Cowper and Newton Museum, Olney,
Buckinghamshire, UK.

ISBN 10: 0-8254-3319-3
ISBN 13: 978-0-8254-3319-1

Printed in the United States of America

07 08 09 10 11 / 6 5 4 3

CONTENTS

PREFACE

For most of us, adventure and terror on the high seas of the eighteenth century is the stuff of historical fiction or costume melodramas. Our closest contact with the sea-faring life is probably a luxury cruise in the Caribbean on what are essentially floating hotels.

One temptation, then, is to dismiss a book written in the late 1700s by a slave-trading sea captain as beyond our experience and interest—until we realize that the sea captain is John Newton, author of the most well known English hymn ever, "Amazing Grace."

While the words of Newton's classic hymn are familiar to most Christians (and even to many non-Christians), Newton's personal story has become less well known over the succeeding centuries. In *Out of the Depths* Newton tells the story, originally in a series of letters, of his prodigal years—without rosy hues or pious halos. For Newton, the depths out of which he came were the depths of sin and depravity. We may wince while singing the words "that saved a wretch like me," but the fault is ours, not the author's. Newton never lost sight of what it meant to be first of all a sinner and secondly an object of God's grace.

The goal of this revised edition has been to provide a balanced text that retains some degree of Newton's eighteenth-century style but with a more contemporary vocabulary and grammar. Newton's writing reflects the reserved and (to modern readers) more formal style of his times. In many places, long sentences containing two, three, or even four clauses have been broken into two or more shorter sentences. In some cases, repetitive adjectives have been combined into one suitable word.

Newton's vocabulary is a challenge to most readers today. For example, when Newton states that "my temper and conduct were exceedingly various," modern readers will benefit from some translation. Newton is likely referring to his habitual disposition or *temperament,* not the "temper" that we so often lose. Nor does he mean that there were "various" *kinds* of temper and conduct; rather, his temperament and conduct were *unstable,* a use of the term now lost in modern English. For decisions such as this, the *Oxford English Dictionary* has been the final authority on usage.

Newton often quotes from or alludes to Scripture passages in his narration, and these have been given reference numbers in parentheses. In a few cases, original text extraneous to the story has been moved to a footnote. Other brief footnotes have been added to define unfamiliar terms, identify persons, or explain incidents unfamiliar today.

My thanks to Dr. Bruce Hindmarsh of Regent College, British Columbia, for his kind assistance in identifying sources for material included in this edition.

—Dennis R. Hillman

Biographical Sketch

John Newton was born in London on July 24, 1725, and he came to occupy a unique position among evangelicals of his time. No doubt the romance of his younger days as well as the force of his character made him the well-known leader he became.

Newton's mother was a devout woman who filled his mind with Scripture, but she died when he was only seven years old. After two years of schooling, during which he learned the basics of Latin, he went to sea with his father. His life out on the deep sea was associated with vivid dreams, sailor recklessness, and remarkable escapes from death. Gradually, he became an abandoned and godless sailor. His father had a heavy heart over the infidelity of his son, who at one time was flogged as a deserter from the British Navy and for over a year lived half-starved and ill-treated in abject degradation under an African slave-dealer. But God, who suddenly confronted another blasphemer, Saul of Tarsus, was about to display His amazing grace in the life of the sinful sailor.

One day John Newton read Thomas à Kempis's *Imitation of Christ;* this sowed the seed of his conversion, which he so vividly describes in his autobiography, now in your hands. At twenty-three years of age, while steering a waterlogged vessel in the face of apparent death, he came to realize his deep need of God. From 1748 through six years, he commanded a slave ship, and in a moment of revelation, turned to God, as he graphically recounts in *Out of the Depths.* Growing in grace, he forsook his sea-life, and for the next nine years he experienced rich and profitable fellowship with renowned revivalists such as John Wesley and George Whitefield.

With a thirst for learning, Newton studied Hebrew and Greek and became a gifted author, giving to the world his *Olney Hymns* (written with the poet William Cowper), *Omicron Letters,* and *Cardiphonia,* which Dr. Alexander Whyte kept on his "selectest shelf of spiritual books." Doubtless, it was his lifelong friendship with William Cowper, the renowned poet, that stimulated his own poetic gift.

In 1780 Newton was appointed Rector of St. Mary Woolnoth Church in London, alongside the Bank of England in the heart of the metropolis. For over twenty years this church was the center of a great widespread evangelical movement. His piety, zeal, warm heart, and candor gained him the friendship of the reformer William Wilberforce, who, through Newton's influence, lead the movement to abolish slavery. In 1805 John Newton's sight failed him and, being unable to read, he was pressed by his friends to retire, but his reply was, "What! shall the old African blasphemer stop when he can speak?"

Two years later, on December 21, 1807, John Newton went to be with the Lord whom he loved and so devotedly served.

—HERBERT LOCKYER

From *Olney Hymns,* 1779
1 Chronicles
Hymn 41
Faith's Review and Expectation
Chap. 18:16, 17

Amazing grace! (how sweet the sound)
    That saved a wretch like me!
I once was lost, but now am found,
    Was blind, but now I see.

'Twas grace that taught my heart to fear,
    And grace my fears relieved;
How precious did that grace appear
    The hour I first believed!

Through many dangers, toils, and snares,
    I have already come;
'Tis grace has brought me safe thus far,
    And grace will lead me home.

The Lord has promised good to me,
    His Word my hope secures;
He will my shield and portion be,
    As long as life endures.

Yes, when this flesh and heart shall fail,
    And mortal life shall cease,
I shall possess, within the vail,
    A life of joy and peace.

The earth shall soon dissolve like snow;
   The sun forbear to shine;
But GOD, who called me here below,
   Will be for ever mine.

1

REASONS FOR WRITING

God's promise to the Israelites is worthy of our reflection. They were then in the wilderness, surrounded with difficulties that were made worse by their distrust and disobedience. They had experienced a variety of God's providential actions, but they did not yet understand God's ultimate goals. They frequently lost sight of God's gracious actions on their behalf and were very discouraged. Moses announces to them that there is a future time of happiness drawing near when their journey and warfare will be finished. They will soon take possession of the Promised Land and rest from all their fears and troubles. Then they will look back with satisfaction upon what was before so difficult to bear: "Thou shalt remember all the way which the Lord thy God led thee through the wilderness" (Deut. 8:2).

The importance and comfort of these words is even greater if we consider them in a spiritual sense. They are addressed to all who are passing through the wilderness of this world to a heavenly Canaan. These travelers, by faith in the promises and power of God, are seeking an eternal rest in that kingdom which cannot be shaken. The hope of that glorious inheritance inspires us with courage and zeal to move forward. When our eyes are fixed upon the Lord, we are more than conquerors over all that may stand in our path.

But we are not there yet. We still feel the weakness and failings of our sinful nature. Because of our own ignorance and unbelief, we often fail to understand the Lord's dealings with us, and we are all too ready to complain. If we knew everything from God's perspective, we would rejoice.

Looking Back

For us, however, there is a time coming when our spiritual warfare will be finished, our perspective enlarged, and our understanding increased. Then we will look back upon the experiences through which the Lord led us and be overwhelmed by adoration and love for Him! We will then see and acknowledge that mercy and goodness directed every step. We shall see that what we once mistakenly called afflictions and misfortune were in reality blessings without which we would not have grown in faith. Nothing happened to us without a reason. No problem came upon us sooner, pressed on us more heavily, or continued longer than our situation required. God, in divine grace and wisdom, used our many afflictions, each as needed, that we might ultimately possess an exceeding and eternal weight of glory, prepared by the Lord for His people.

We very often fail to see our present circumstances in right perspective. Look back over the past, however, and compare what you have been brought through with your frame of mind during each successive period. Consider how wonderfully one thing has been connected with another so that what we now count as our greatest benefits are rooted in incidents that at the time seemed insignificant. We have sometimes escaped from grave dangers not by any wisdom or foresight of our own, but by the intervention of unforeseen circumstances. So both the revelation of Scripture and our own individual experiences confirm the wisdom and good providence of God. He watches over His people from the earliest moment of their lives. He overrules and guards them through all their blind wanderings and leads them in a way that they know not.

God's Wise and Good Providence

I am persuaded that every believer will see enough in his or her own life to confirm this, but not all in the same degree. The outward circumstances of many Christians appear the same. They have not been through extreme circumstances of one kind or another. Inwardly, a spiritual change has been effected without notice by others and almost unperceived by themselves. The Lord has spoken to them, not in thunder and tempest, but with a still small voice He has drawn them gradually to Himself. Although they have a confident assurance that they know and love Him and have passed from death unto life, they cannot relate any great details of a drastic change.

Others He seems to select in order to show the exceeding riches of His grace and the greatness of His mighty power. He allows the natural rebellion and wickedness of their hearts to completely express itself. Even though they sin willfully against God, they are spared from death while other sinners are cut off with little warning. Just when all who know them are expecting to hear that God has brought down divine vengeance upon them, the Lord, (whose thoughts are high above ours, as the heavens are higher than the earth) is pleased to pluck them like brands out of the fire. He makes them monuments of His mercy for the encouragement of others. They are—contrary to expectation—convinced, pardoned, and changed.

When this happens, it demonstrates a divine power equal to the same divine power seen in the creation of a world. It is without question the Lord's doing, and it is marvelous to all those who are not blinded by prejudice and unbelief.

Saul of Tarsus

Saul was full of blind hatred for Jesus of Nazareth, so he persecuted His disciples and tried to destroy them. He had terrorized the church in Jerusalem and was going to Damascus for the same purpose. He was "breathing out threatenings and slaughter" against all who loved the Lord Jesus (Acts 9:1). He gave little thought to the violence he had done and was determined to suppress the whole sect. He moved from house to house and from place to place, his face a mask of intimidation and every word a threat.

The Lord Jesus, whom Saul hated and opposed, checked him at the height of his rage. The Lord called him from being a fierce persecutor to the high honor of being an apostle, and inspired him to preach, with great zeal and earnestness, the very faith which he so recently had sought to destroy.[1]

His Own Example

In connection with such a person, permit me to add my own name. Saul was once an eminent sinner but proved himself to be an eminent Christian. He had been forgiven much and he loved much. As Paul, he could say, "The grace bestowed upon me was not in vain; for I labored more abundantly than they all" (1 Cor. 15:10).

It has not been that way with me. I feel a well-deserved shame that I have not made the most of what I have received. However, in light of the patience and longsuffering of God, the wonderful interposition of His providence in favor of an unworthy sinner, the power of His grace in softening the hardest of hearts, and the riches of His mercy in pardoning my enormous and aggravated transgressions—in these respects I know no case more extraordinary than mine. Most of those who have heard my story think that it is worthy of being preserved.

The First Letters

I was reluctant to write my story—on the one hand, because it is difficult to write objectively whenever "self" is concerned; on the other, because of the misuse which persons of corrupt and perverse minds are often known to make of such stories.[2] The psalmist reminds us that caution in these things is proper: "Come and hear, all ye that fear God, and I will declare what he hath done for my soul" (Ps. 66:16) and our Lord cautions us not to "cast pearls before swine" (Matt. 7:6). The pearls of a Christian are, perhaps, his choice experiences of the Lord's power and love in regards to his soul. These should not casually be made public, lest we provide an occasion for disreputable persons to make fun of what they cannot understand.

I yielded to the request of a much-respected friend and sent him my story in a series of eight letters. Although I wrote to this one person, my letters have passed into many hands. As my friends will understand, I was willing to share my story if my compliance with this request may result in some good effect, may promote the pleasing work of praise to our adorable Redeemer, or confirm the faith of some of His people. If God may be glorified by my efforts and His children in any measure be comforted or instructed by what I have to declare of His goodness, I shall be satisfied. I am content to leave all other possible consequences of this undertaking in His hands.

A More Explicit Narrative

Since I retained no copies of my letters, I must again make use of memory.[3] I hope readers will excuse me if I do not confine myself to only a narration of events, but now and then intersperse my own reflections with my writing. I shall, however, write as much as possible with the confidence and freedom that friendship and honesty deserve.

Endnotes

1. Newton here mentions a Colonel Gardiner, whom he describes as follows: "There are also remarkable displays of the same sovereign, efficacious grace in our own times. I particularly mention the instance of the late Colonel Gardiner. If any real satisfaction could be found in a sinful course, he would have met with it. He pursued the experiment with all possible advantages. He was habituated to evil; and many uncommon, almost miraculous, deliverances made no impression on him. Yet he was made willing in the day of God's power; and the bright example of his life, has afforded an occasion of much praise to God, and much comfort to His people." And later: "Colonel Gardiner was as a city set upon a hill, a burning and a shining light; the manner of his conversion was hardly

more singular than the whole course of his conversation from that time to his death." Colonel James Gardiner (1688–1745) was killed in battle after a heroic stand in which he was deserted by most of his men. His miraculous conversion after a dissolute life was commemorated in his biography by Philip Dodderidge.

2. Newton's original story was told in eight letters that he later expanded, upon request of an interested reader, to fourteen letters. These were finally published in 1764, shortly after his thirty-ninth birthday, under the title *An Authentic Narrative of Some Remarkable Particulars in the Life of* *******.

3. Newton's original eight letters were written to Thomas Haweis, a hospital chaplain in London.

2

YOUTHFUL DAYS

How pleasing it is to repeat the confession of David, "O Lord, I am Thy servant, the son of Thine handmaid; Thou hast loosed my bonds" (Ps. 116:16). God's tender mercies on my behalf were clearly seen in the first moments of my life. It was as if I was born in His house and dedicated to Him in my infancy. Many people have told me that my mother was a devout and mature Christian, a member of the Dissenting church.[1] She was not physically strong and had a reserved personality. I was her only child and almost all of her attention was given to my education. I have some faint recollections of her care and instructions. When I was about three years of age, she herself taught me to read. When I was four years old, I could read any common book with understanding. She helped me store in my memory, which was then very retentive, many valuable verses, portions, and chapters of Scripture as well as catechisms, hymns, and poems.

Encouragement for Parents

During my early years I had little interest in the noisy sports of children. I was most happy in my mother's company and was always as willing to learn as she was to teach. Even the best education may fall short of affecting the heart, as my own story will demonstrate; but I think my example should be an encouragement for godly parents to continue doing their part faithfully. Although in later years I sinned away all the advantages of my early learning, they did restrain my behavior for some time. They returned in my mind again and again, and it was a very long time before I could wholly shake them off. When the Lord finally opened my eyes, I found that my recollection of them was a great benefit. My dear mother, besides the care she took with me, often commended me to God with many prayers and tears.

My mother noted my early progress with great satisfaction and planned from my earliest years to prepare me for the ministry, if the Lord should so incline my heart. In my sixth year I began to learn Latin, but before I had time to learn much of the language, the intended plan of my education was interrupted. I was deprived of my mother when I was not quite seven years old. I was born July 24, 1725, and she died July 11, 1732.[2] The Lord's designs were far beyond the plans of an earthly parent. He chose to use me as an unusual proof of His patience, providence, and grace.

My father was at sea. He was a commander in the Mediterranean trade at that time. He came home the following year and soon after married again. I was then given into the care of others. I was well treated, but there was no remedy for the loss of my mother's instruction. I was now permitted to mingle with negligent and irreligious children, and I soon began to imitate their conduct.

Soon after my father's marriage, I was sent to a boarding school in Essex. The school master's ill-advised harshness almost broke my spirit and my enthusiasm for books. While there I forgot the first principles and rules of arithmetic, which my mother had taught me years before. I stayed for two years, but in the second year a new teacher came who observed and took into account my temperament. I took to Latin with great eagerness, and before I was ten years old I could read Latin authors such as Virgil.

I believe I was pushed forward too fast, however. Not being grounded, I soon lost all I had learned, and I left school in my tenth year. Years later when I studied Latin from books, I think I had little, if any, advantage from my early learning.

Early Sea Voyages

When I was eleven years old, my father took me to sea with him. A man of great practical sense and experience in the world, he was careful to protect my morals; but he could not make up for my mother's absence. Having been educated in Spain, he always maintained a sense of distance and sternness in his manner that intimidated and discouraged me. I was always in fear of him, and therefore he had less of an influence upon my life.

From 1736 to 1742 I made several voyages, spending considerable intervals between voyages in the country. Shortly after my fifteenth birthday I was given a very promising position at Alicant, Spain; but my undisciplined behavior and rebelliousness ruined the opportunity.

During this period my disposition and conduct were exceedingly unstable. I had little concern for religion and was easily angered. However I was often disturbed by my conscience. I had enjoyed reading since my childhood. Among other books, I found Benet's *Christian Oratory*. Although I only understood a little of

When I was eleven years old my father took me to sea with him.

it, the course of life it recommended appeared very desirable. I decided to attempt it. I began to pray, to read the Scriptures, and to keep a diary.

Soon I felt that I was "religious." This seeming goodness, however, had no solid foundation and soon passed away like a morning cloud or the early dew. I was soon tired of the effort, gradually gave it up, and finally became worse than before. Instead of prayer, I learned to curse and blaspheme and was very sinful when not under my parent's supervision.

Before I was twelve years old, I had a dangerous fall from a horse. I was thrown, unhurt, within a few inches of a newly trimmed hedgerow.[3] I could not avoid recognizing God's gracious providence in my deliverance. Had I fallen upon the stakes I likely would have been killed. My conscience reminded me of the dreadful consequences had I been summoned to appear before God in my godless condition.

I subsequently broke off my sinful practices and appeared quite altered; but it was not long before I succumbed to them again. This struggle between sin and conscience was repeated often, and every relapse sank me into still greater depths of wickedness.

Once I was moved by the death of a close companion. We had agreed to go on board a war ship (I think it was on a Sunday); but I providentially arrived too late. The boat overturned, and my friend and several others drowned. At my friend's funeral I was overwhelmed by the thought that due to a delay of just a few minutes (which had angered me), my life had been preserved. However, this also was soon forgotten.

Another time my reading of the *Family Instructor* started me on a partial and brief reformation. Although I cannot distinctly recall the specifics, I think I took up and laid aside a religious profession three or four different times before I was sixteen years old. During all of this time my heart was insincere.

I understood the necessity of religion as a means of escaping hell, but I loved sin and was unwilling to forsake it. There were frequent instances of this stubbornness, and I was strangely blind and stupid. Sometimes when I determined to do things that I knew were sinful and contrary to my moral duty, I could not continue untroubled until I first performed my routine of prayer. I begrudged every moment of such time; but when it was finished, my conscience was in some measure pacified, and I could rush into foolishness with little remorse.

My last effort at reform was the most remarkable in its thoroughness and continuance. I might describe this period with the apostle Paul's words, "After the straitest sect of our religion I lived a Pharisee" (Phil. 3:5). I did everything that might be expected from a person entirely ignorant of God's righteousness who works to build his own self-righteousness. I spent the majority of every day in the reading of Scripture, in meditation, and in prayer. I fasted often. I even abstained from all meat for three months. I would hardly answer a question for fear of speaking a wrong word. I seemed to regret my former misconduct very earnestly, sometimes with tears.

I became an ascetic and attempted, so far as my position would permit, to give up all social contacts so that I might avoid temptation. I continued in this serious mood (I cannot give it a higher title) for more than two years without any relaxing of my efforts. It was a poor religion that left me, in many respects, under the power of sin. It tended to make me depressed, apathetic, unsociable, and useless.

Such was my frame of mind when I became acquainted with

Lord Shaftesbury's *Characteristics*.[4] The title attracted me, and I enjoyed the writing, especially the second piece entitled "A Rhapsody." Nothing could be more suited to my romantic mind than this pompous discourse. I thought that the author was a most religious person and that I had only to follow him and be happy.

Thus, with fine words and fair speeches, my simple heart was beguiled. This book was always in my hand, and I read it until I could very nearly repeat the "Rhapsody" verbatim from beginning to end. No immediate effect followed; but it operated like a slow poison and prepared the way for all that came after.

In December 1742 I returned from a voyage, and my father, thinking of not sending me to sea again, considered how to settle me in the world. I had little enthusiasm for business, and I knew very little of the world. I was fond of a visionary contemplative life, a medley of religion, philosophy, and laziness. I was quite averse to the thought of an industrious application to business.

Finally a merchant in Liverpool, a close friend of my father's (to whom, as the instrument of God's goodness, I owe for all my earthly comforts), proposed to send me for some years to Jamaica and to take upon himself the responsibility for my future.[5] I agreed to this and was on the point of setting out the following week. In the meantime my father sent me on some business a few miles beyond Maidstone in Kent. This short journey, which was to have been only for three or four days, occasioned a sudden and remarkable change, which roused me from my indolence. "The way of man is not in himself; it is not in man that walketh to direct his steps" (Jer. 10:23).

Endnotes

1. Christians who refused to participate in the state church or Church of England. The term was originally applied to both Roman Catholics and Puritans who refused to give their allegiance to the Church of England under Elizabeth I. Later it came to apply to numerous Protestant groups.
2. Newton's mother died of tuberculosis after being cared for at the home of her longtime friend, Elizabeth Catlett. Spread easily in the crowded housing of London and without medical cure, tuberculosis was routinely fatal.
3. No doubt Newton would have been impaled upon the sharpened ends of the hedge.
4. The works of Anthony Cooper, third earl of Shaftesbury (1671–1713). Cooper's writings, published in three volumes in 1711, reflected his education under philosopher John Locke and stressed a natural inclination to virtue or an innate "moral sense" in every person. Thus a person's natural virtue would override selfish inclinations. Cooper followed the Church of England, but in his writings held that atheism was an acceptable belief. Cooper himself was a Deist who rejected the Bible as a divine revelation and discounted miracles as a subversion of the natural order.
5. Joseph Manesty, former ship's captain, now merchant and ship's owner in the African slave trade, would be Newton's friend and future employer in the slave trade.

3

EARLY LIFE AS A SAILOR

A few days before my intended journey, I received an invitation to visit very close friends of my mother in Kent. Because of their coolness toward my father's second marriage, I had heard nothing from them for many years.

I obtained my father's permission to call on them, but I was very indifferent about it and sometimes thought of not going. However, I went. I was known at first sight and given the kindest reception as the child of their dear, deceased friend.

My mother's friends had two daughters. The eldest, as I learned some years later, had been considered by her mother and mine as a future wife for me from the time of her birth. I do not say that my mother predicted what was to happen, yet there was something remarkable in how it took place.

All communication between the families had been long broken off; I was going into a foreign country and only intended to pay a hasty visit. I would not have thought of such a visit since I had not been invited before. The invitation had arrived at a crucial point in my life, and the circumstances of my visit were certainly unusual and unexpected.

His Future Wife

Almost at the first sight of this girl (for she was then under fourteen), I felt an affection for her that never abated or lost its influence a single moment in my heart.[1] In degree, it equaled all that the writers of romance have imagined; in duration it was unalterable.

I would later lose all sense of religion and become deaf to the promptings of conscience. None of the misery I experienced ever banished her from my waking thoughts for a single hour in the following seven years.

Hardly anything less than this intense and compelling passion would have been sufficient to awaken me from the dull melancholy habit I had formed. Even though I greatly admired the pictures of virtue and benevolence drawn by Lord Shaftesbury, I almost despised others; but now my desire to withdraw from life was overcome. I was willing to be or to do anything that might accomplish my wishes at some future time.

Restraining Effect of Love

When I later made shipwreck of faith, hope, and conscience, my love for this person was the only remaining principle which in any degree took their place. The bare possibility of seeing her again was the only means of restraining me from the most horrible actions against myself and others.

But the ill effects it brought counterbalanced these advantages. Courtship is indeed a pleasing part of life when there is mutual affection, the consent of friends, the reasonable prospect of an eventual fulfillment, and when it is conducted in obedience to the will and worship of God. But when these concomitants are absent, what we call love becomes the most tormenting and destructive passion that can be named.

And they were all lacking in my case. I dared not mention it to her friends or to my own nor for a considerable time to her since I could make no proposals. The conflict remained as a dark fire, locked up in my heart, which gave me constant uneasiness. It greatly weakened my sense of religion and opened the way for the entrance of ungodly beliefs. My love seemed to promise great things as an incentive to diligence and activity in life; but in reality it performed nothing. I often considered what I would willingly do or suffer for the sake of her I loved; yet I was incapable of forcing myself away from her company to improve my opportunities.

It did not prevent me from engaging in a long period of excess and revelry, utterly unworthy of my honorable pretensions. Through the wonderful intervention of divine goodness, the maze of my follies was at length unraveled; yet I am sure I would not go through the same series of trouble again even if it gained me all the treasures of the Indies.

I now considered everything in a new light. I concluded it would be absolutely impossible to live as far away as Jamaica for a term of four or five years. Therefore I determined that I would not go. I could not bear either to tell my father the true reason or to invent a false one; therefore, without giving any notice to him why I did so, I stayed three weeks instead of three days in Kent. I thought the opportunity would be lost, and the ship would have sailed.

I then returned to London. I had highly displeased my father by this disobedience; but he was more easily reconciled than I expected. In a little time I sailed with a friend of his to Venice. On this voyage I was exposed to the company and bad example of the common sailors, among whom I was classed. With opportunities presenting themselves every day, I once more began to relax from the sobriety and control that I had observed in some degree for more than two years.

I was sometimes pierced with sharp convictions. Though I made a few faint efforts to stop, I never recovered from this decline as I had from several before. I did not as yet become completely degenerate, but I was making large strides toward total apostasy from God. The most remarkable warning I received (and the last) was a dream, which made a very strong, although not abiding, impression on my mind.

His Dream of the Ring

In my dream the scene was the harbor of Venice, where we had lately been. I thought it was night, and I was standing my watch upon the dock. As I was walking back and forth by myself, someone brought me a ring. I was explicitly charged to keep it carefully and assured that while I preserved that ring I would be happy and successful. If I lost or parted with it, I must expect nothing but trouble and misery. I accepted the present and the terms willingly, not doubting in the least that I would carefully preserve it. I was highly satisfied to have my happiness in my own keeping.

Then a second person came to me. Observing the ring on my finger, he began to ask some questions concerning it. I readily told him about its virtues. He expressed surprise at my weakness in expecting such effects from a ring. He reasoned with me for some time and at last urged me to throw the ring away.

At first I was shocked at the proposal, but his persuasions prevailed. I began to think and then to doubt. At last I plucked it off my finger and dropped it over the ship's side into the water. At the same instant, a terrible fire burst out from a range of the mountains, a part of the Alps, which appeared at some distance behind the city of Venice. I saw the hills as distinctly as if awake, and they were all in flames.

I perceived, too late, my foolishness. My tempter, with an air of insult, informed me that all the mercy of God in reserve for me was contained in that ring, which I had willfully thrown away. I understood that I must now go with him to the burning mountains, and that all the flames I saw were kindled on my account. I trembled, and was in a great agony, but my dream continued. As I stood self-condemned, without plea or hope, suddenly a third person, or the same who brought the ring at first (I am not certain which), came to me and asked for the cause of my grief.

I told him plainly, confessing that I had ruined myself willfully and deserved no pity. He blamed my foolhardiness and asked if I would be wiser if I had my ring again. I could hardly answer for I thought it was gone beyond recovery. Indeed, I had no time to answer before I saw this unexpected friend go down under the water, just at the spot where I had dropped the ring. He soon returned, bringing it with him.

The moment he came on board, the flames in the mountains were extinguished and my seducer left me. Then was "the prey taken from the hand of the mighty, and the lawful captive delivered" (Isa. 49:24). My fears ended, and with joy and gratitude I approached my kind deliverer to receive my ring again. But he refused to return it and said to me, "If you are to be entrusted with this ring again, you would very soon bring yourself into the same distress. You are not able to keep it, but I will preserve it for you. Whenever it is needful, I will produce it in your behalf."

I awoke in a state of mind that is difficult to describe. I could hardly eat, sleep, or transact my necessary business for two or three days. The impression soon wore off, however, and I totally forgot it. It hardly occurred to my mind again until several years later.

A time came when I found myself in circumstances closely resembling those suggested by this extraordinary dream, and I stood helpless and hopeless upon the brink of an awful eternity. Had the eyes of my mind been opened then, I would have seen my grand enemy, who had seduced me willfully to renounce and throw away my religious professions and to involve myself in a tangle of sin. I probably should have seen his pleasure with my agonies, his waiting for permission to steal my soul away to his place of torment.

I should perhaps have seen likewise that Jesus, whom I had persecuted and defied, rebuking the adversary, claiming me for His own as a brand plucked out of the fire and saying, "Deliver him from going down to the pit: I have found a ransom."

Although I did not see these things, I found the benefit. I obtained mercy. The Lord answered me in the day of my distress, and, blessed be His name, He who restored the ring (or what was signified by it) promises to keep it. Oh, what an unspeakable comfort is this, that I am not my own keeper! "The Lord is my Shepherd." I have been enabled to trust my all into His hands, and I know whom I have believed. Satan still desires to have me, that he might sift me as wheat, but my Savior has prayed for me that my faith may not fail.

Here is my security and power, a bulwark against which the gates of hell cannot prevail. But for this, many a time and often, if possible, I would have ruined myself following my first deliverance. Moreover, I would fall and stumble and perish still, after all that the Lord has done for me, if His faithfulness were not engaged on my behalf to be my Sun and Shield, even unto death. "Bless the Lord, O my soul."

Nothing very remarkable occurred in the following part of that voyage. I returned home in December 1743 and soon after repeated my visit to Kent where I protracted my stay in the same careless manner as before. This again disappointed my father and almost provoked him to disown me.

On Board a Man-of-War

Before anything suitable presented itself again, I was pressed into service, owing entirely to my own thoughtless conduct, and put on board a supply ship.[2] It was at a critical juncture when the French fleets were hovering on our coast so my father was unable to procure my release. In a few days I was sent on board the *Harwich*. I entered here upon quite a new experience of life and endured much hardship for about a month.[3]

My father felt that I should remain in the navy since a war was daily expected and procured a recommendation to the captain, who took me upon the quarter-deck as a midshipman. I had now an easy life and might have gained respect, but my mind was unsettled and my behavior very apathetic. I met with companions who completed the ruin of my principles. I pretended to talk of virtue and was not so outwardly abandoned as afterward, yet my delight and habitual practice was wickedness.

My closest companion was a person of many natural talents and a keen mind. He was very skilled in what is called the "free-thinking" scheme[4] and knew how to state his beliefs in the most plausible way. He could hardly have labored more in the cause if he had expected to gain heaven by it. This man, whom I honored as my master and whose practice I adopted so eagerly, was overtaken in a voyage to Lisbon by a violent storm. The vessel and people escaped, but a great wave broke over the ship and swept him into eternity. Thus the Lord spares or punishes, according to His sovereign pleasure.

I was fond of his company and having myself a smattering of books, I was eager enough to show my reading. He soon perceived that I had not wholly broken through the restraints of conscience and therefore did not shock me at first with a complete disclosure of his beliefs. Instead, he spoke favorably of religion, but when he had gained my confidence, he began to speak more plainly. Perceiving my ignorant attachment to the *Characteristics,* he took issue with me concerning that book and convinced me that I had never understood it.

He confronted me with so many objections and arguments that my depraved heart was soon overcome, and I entered into his plan with all my heart. Thus like an unwary sailor, who leaves his port just before a rising storm, I renounced the hopes and comforts of the gospel at the very time when every other comfort was about to fail me.

In December 1744, the *Harwich* was in port, soon to be bound for the East Indies. The captain gave me liberty to go on shore for a day. Imprudently disregarding consequences, I took off on horseback. Following the dictates of my restless passion, I desired to take a last leave of the one I loved. I had little satisfaction in the visit since I was conscious that I was taking pains to merely multiply my own troubles. The short time I could stay passed like a dream, and on New Year's Day, 1745, I returned to the ship. The captain was prevailed on to excuse my absence. But this rash step, especially since it was not the first liberty I had taken, highly displeased him and lost me his favor, which I never recovered.

Finally we sailed with a very large fleet. We put into Torbay due to a change of wind; but turning fair again, we sailed the next day. Several of our fleet were lost in attempting to leave that place. The following night the whole fleet was greatly endangered on the coast of Cornwall by a storm from the southward. The darkness of the night and the number of the vessels resulted in much confusion and damage. Our ship, though several times in imminent danger of being run down by other vessels, escaped unhurt. Many others, however, were damaged, particularly the *Admiral*. This occasioned our putting back to Plymouth.

While we lay in harbor at Plymouth, I heard that my father, who had interest in some of the ships lately lost, had come down to Torbay. He had a connection at that time with the African Company. I thought that if I could get to him, he might easily introduce me into that service, which would be better than pursuing a long, uncertain voyage to the East Indies.

It was a maxim with me, in those unhappy days, never to deliberate. The thought hardly occurred to me before I resolved to leave the ship in any case. I did so, and in the worst manner possible. I was sent one day in the landing boat to take care that none of the crew deserted. But I betrayed my trust and went off myself. I did not know what road to take and dared not ask for fear of being suspected. Having some general idea of the country,

I guessed right. When I had traveled some miles, I made an inquiry and found that I was on the road to Dartmouth.

All went smoothly that day and part of the next. I had expected to be with my father in about two hours when a small party of soldiers met me. I could not avoid or deceive them. They brought me back to Plymouth and walked me through the streets guarded like a felon. My heart was full of indignation, shame, and fear. I was confined for two days in the guardhouse and then sent on board my ship. I was kept awhile in iron shackles, then publicly stripped and whipped, after which I was degraded from my office.[5] All my former companions were forbidden to show me the least favor or even to speak to me. As a midshipman I had been entitled to some command. Being haughty and vain, I had not been bashful in exerting authority. I was now brought down to a level with the lowest seaman and exposed to the insults of all.

My present situation was uncomfortable; my future prospects were even worse. The misfortunes I suffered were likely to grow heavier every day. In the early days of my catastrophe, the officers and my former shipmates attempted to screen me from mistreatment; but during the short time I remained with them afterwards, I found they cooled very fast in their endeavors to protect me. Indeed they could not avoid it without running a great risk of sharing punishment with me. The captain, though in general a humane man who behaved very well to the ship's crew, was almost implacable in his resentment when he had been greatly offended. He took several occasions to demonstrate his resentment of me, and the voyage was to last for five years.

I think nothing I either felt or feared distressed me so much as being thus forcibly torn away from the object of my affections under a great improbability of seeing her again. It seemed equally improbable that I would return in such a manner as would give me hopes of making her mine. Thus I was as miserable in every way that could be imagined. My heart was filled with the most excruciating passions, eager desire, bitter rage, and black despair. Every hour exposed me to some new insult and hardship, with no hope of relief or mitigation, no friend to take my part or to listen to my complaint.

Inwardly or outwardly I could perceive nothing but darkness and misery. I think no case, except that of a conscience wounded by the wrath of God, could be more dreadful than mine. I cannot express with what wishfulness and regret I cast my last look upon the English shore. I kept my eyes fixed upon it until it disappeared. When I could no longer see it, I was tempted to throw myself into the sea. According to the atheistic system I had adopted, this would put an end to all my sorrows at once. But the secret hand of God restrained me.

Endnotes

1. Newton regularly mentions his affection for Mary Catlett through all his ensuing difficulties, although he rarely uses her actual name, preferring terms such as "my beloved."
2. "Pressured" is the term Newton uses, in the sense of being "pressed" or forced to serve in the navy. Unfortunate victims of the "press gang" were abducted and forced to serve in the Royal Navy for an indefinite term. This happened in February, 1744. Newton would be nineteen years old the following summer.
3. The *Harwich* was a newly commissioned 976-ton warship with a crew of 350 men.
4. Rationalist philosophy that sought to explain everything by reason and natural causes without resorting to supernatural revelation.

5. Newton probably received twelve lashes, the maximum allowed without a court martial. Such a flogging left the back severely lacerated. Salt water was poured on the wounds before the victim was wrapped with bandages.

4

VOYAGE TO AFRICA

When I began this series of letters, I intended to say no more of myself than might be necessary to illustrate the wonders of divine providence and grace in my life; but I was later encouraged to expand upon my original plan.

Among other things I was asked for a more detailed account of my courtship. On this point I thought it was fitting for me to be very brief, but I complied with my readers' wishes. This seems to be a proper place to tell you how things stood when I left England.

When my attraction to my beloved was first evident, both of us were so young that no one but myself considered it seriously. It served for tea table talk among our friends, and nothing further was expected from it. My love seemed to have abiding effects so that in two years it had not let up. It especially caused me to act without any regard to prudence or self-interest or my father's plans (there continued a coolness between him and the family). As a result, her parents began to consider our eventual marriage as a matter of consequence.

When I took my last leave of them, her mother expressed the most tender affection for me, as if I had been her own child. She told me that she had no objections to our engagement at a more mature age and with a settled future in view. Yet as things then stood, she thought herself obliged to interfere. She therefore wished that I would not think of returning to their house, unless her daughter was away from home, until such time as I could either entirely give up my intentions or I could assure her that I had my father's express consent to continue.

It was a difficult parting, but even though she was young, light-hearted, and quite unpracticed in such matters, she was directed to take a pleasant but neutral position towards me. A positive encouragement or an absolute refusal would have both posed equal, though different, disadvantages. But without much study on her part, she was always upon her guard. She had insight to see her absolute power over me and the good sense to make a proper use of it. She would neither understand my hints nor give me room to come to a direct explanation. She said that from the first discovery of my regard for her, and long before, the thought was agreeable to her. Therefore, she had often an unaccountable impression that sooner or later she should be mine. Upon these terms we parted.

No Fear of God Before His Eyes

I return to my voyage. During our passage to Madeira, I fell prey to the most depressed thoughts. Although I well deserved all I met with and the captain might have been justified if he had carried his resentment still further, yet my pride at that time suggested that I had been terribly insulted. This so worked upon my wicked heart that I actually formed plans to kill him. This was one reason that made me willing to prolong my own life. I was sometimes divided between killing the captain and killing myself, not thinking it practicable to carry out both plans.

The Lord had now, to all appearances, given me up to a hardness of heart under His judgment. I was capable of anything. I had not the least fear of God before my eyes, nor, so far as I remember, the least sensibility of conscience. I was possessed by so strong a spirit of delusion that I believed my own lie and was firmly persuaded that after death I should cease to be. Yet the Lord preserved me! Some moments of sober reflection would at times take place. When I had chosen death rather than life, a ray of hope would come in. There was little probability, however, for a hope that I would yet see better days and that I might again return to England and have my wishes crowned, that is if I did not willfully throw life away.

My love was now the only restraint I had left. Though I neither feared God nor regarded men, I could not bear that she should think poorly of me when I was dead. In the outward concerns of life, divine providence often employs the weakest means to produce great effects beyond their common influence, for instance, when a disease is removed by a fright.

Such means I found then. This single thought, which had not restrained me from a thousand smaller evils, proved my only and effectual barrier against the greatest and most fatal temptations. How long I could have maintained this conflict or what, humanly speaking, would have been the consequences of my continuing in that situation, I cannot say. The Lord, whom I seldom thought of, knew my danger and was providing for my deliverance.

Discharged from *H.M.S. Harwich*

I had determined two things while at Plymouth: that I would not go to India and that I would go to Guinea. Such indeed was the Lord's will concerning me, but they were to be accomplished in His way, not in mine.

We had been at Madeira some time. The business of the fleet was completed, and we were to sail the following day. On that memorable morning I was late in bed. I would have slept longer, but one of the midshipmen, an old companion, came down below decks, and between jest and earnestness urged me to get up. Since I did not immediately comply, he cut down the hammock in which I lay, which forced me to dress. I was very angry, but dared not resent it. I was little aware how much his whim would affect me! This person, who had no plan in what he did, was the messenger of God's providence. I said little, but went upon deck, where I that moment saw a man putting his clothes into a boat. He told me he was going to leave us. Upon inquiring, I was informed that two men, from a Guinea ship, which lay near us, had entered on board the *Harwich,* and that the commodore, Sir George Pocock, had ordered the captain to send two others in their place.

My heart instantly burned like fire. I begged for the boat to be detained a few minutes. I ran to the lieutenant and begged him to intercede with the captain that I might be dismissed. Although I had been formerly upon ill terms with these officers and had crossed them all at one time or another, yet they had pitied my case and were ready to help me now. When we were at Plymouth, the captain had refused to exchange me at the request of Admiral Medley but was now easily prevailed on. In little more than

Since I did not immediately comply, he cut down the hammock in which I lay. . . .

half an hour from my being asleep in bed, I was discharged and safe on board another ship.

This was one of the many critical turns of my life in which the Lord was pleased to display His providence and care by causing many unexpected circumstances to concur in almost an instant of time. These sudden opportunities were several times repeated. Each of them brought me into an entirely new scene of action, and they were usually delayed to almost the last possible moment in which they could have taken place.

Sinning with a High Hand

The ship I went on board was bound for Sierra Leone and the adjacent parts of what is called the Windward Coast of Africa.[1] The commander, I found, was acquainted with my father. He received me very kindly and offered seemingly sincere promises of assistance. I believe he would have been my friend, but without learning the least lesson from my former mistakes and troubles, I pursued the same course. If possible, I acted much worse.

On board the *Harwich*, though my principles were totally corrupted, at first I was in some degree sedate and serious. Now, entering among strangers, I could appear without disguise. I well remember that while I was passing from the one ship to the other, this was one reason why I rejoiced in the exchange. One reflection I made upon the occasion was "that I now might be as abandoned as I pleased, without any control." From this time I was exceedingly wretched indeed, little if anything short of that animated description of an almost irrecoverable state which we have in 2 Peter 2:14.[2]

I not only sinned with a high hand myself, but made it my study to tempt and seduce others upon every occasion. I eagerly sought such occasions, sometimes to my own hazard and hurt. One natural consequence of this was a loss of favor with my new captain. Not that he was at all religious or disliked my wickedness, but I became careless and disobedient. I did not please him because I did not intend to, and since he had an odd temper likewise, we the more easily disagreed. Besides, I had a little of that unlucky wit that can multiply troubles and enemies to its possessor. Upon some imagined affront, I made up a song in which I ridiculed his ship, his command, and his person. I soon taught it to the whole ship's company. Such was the ungrateful return I made for his offers of friendship and protection. I had mentioned no names, but the allusion was plain, and he was no stranger either to the intention or the author. I shall say no more of this part of my story; let it be buried in eternal silence.

But let me not fail to praise that grace which could pardon, that blood which could expiate, such sins as mine. Yea, "the Ethiopian may change his skin, and the leopard his spots" (Jer.13:23). I, who was the willing slave of every evil, possessed with a legion of unclean spirits, have been spared, saved, and changed, to stand as a monument of His almighty power forever.

Thus I went on for about six months, by which time the ship was preparing to leave the coast. A few days before she sailed, the captain died. I was not upon much better terms with his mate who now succeeded to the command, and he had upon some occasions treated me ill. I had no doubt that if I went with him to the West Indies, he would put me on board a man-of-war. This, from what I had known already, was more dreadful to me than death. To avoid it, I determined to remain in Africa and amused myself with many golden dreams that here I should find an opportunity of improving my fortune.

Enters the Slave Trade

There are only a few white men settled upon that part of the coast now. There were many more at the time I was first there. Their business it was to purchase slaves along the adjacent rivers and countryside and to sell them to the ships at an advanced price.

One of these men, who had landed in Africa indigent like myself, had acquired considerable wealth. He had recently been in England and was returning in the vessel I was in (of which he owned a quarter share). His example impressed me with hopes of the same success, and upon condition of entering into his service, I obtained my discharge from the ship. I did not take the precaution of agreeing upon terms of employment, but trusted his generosity. I received no compensation for my time on board the ship, only a bill due the owners in England. This was never paid since they went out of business before my return to England. The day the vessel sailed, I landed upon Banana Island with little more than the clothes upon my back, as if I had escaped shipwreck.[3]

Endnotes

1. Leaving the Royal Navy, Newton was now exposed to the realities of the African slave trade firsthand. This ship was not named by Newton but was probably the *Levant*, a 200-ton slave vessel commanded by James Phelps.

2. "... having eyes full of adultery, and that cannot cease from sin; beguiling unstable souls: an heart they have exercised with covetous practices; cursed children" (KJV). Some contemporaries of Newton suggested that he exaggerated the extent of his "wickedness." While Newton never explicitly says so, he hints here and in his other writings that he engaged in sexual relations with female slaves. He wrote elsewhere of the predatory lust of the sailors for female slaves. He would later tell a friend that he was "a slave to every customary vice."

3. Newton and his new, unnamed master would end up on Plantain Island, two miles off the coast of today's Sierra Leone.

5

TRIALS IN WEST AFRICA

There is an important instruction in the words of our Lord, "Mine hour is not yet come" (John 2:4). The following two years, of which I now give some account, will seem as an absolute blank in a very short life. But as the Lord's hour of grace had not yet come, I was to have still deeper experiences of the dreadful state of the heart of man when left to itself. I have since frequently admired the mercy of the Lord in banishing me to those distant parts and almost excluding me from human society at a time when I was filled with sinfulness. Like one infected with a pestilence, I was capable of spreading a taint wherever I went.

Had my affairs taken a different turn, had I succeeded in my plans and remained in England, my sad story would probably have been worse. I could hardly have been worse as a person, but my wickedness would have had greater scope. I might have been very hurtful to others and multiplied irreparable evils. But the Lord wisely placed me where I could do others little harm. The few I had to converse with were also much like myself, and I was soon brought into such abject circumstances that I was too low to have any influence. I was rather shunned and despised than imitated. Most persons, even among the Negroes, thought themselves too good to speak to me during the first year of my residence among them.

I was as yet an "outcast lying in my blood" (Ezek. 16:6), and to all appearance, exposed to perish. But the Lord looked at me with mercy. He did not strike me down to hell, as I justly deserved. "He passed by me when I was in my blood, and said unto me, Live" (16:6). The appointed time for the manifestation of His love that covered all my iniquities with the robe of His righteousness and admitted me to the privileges of His children was not until long afterwards. Yet He still urged me to live. I can only ascribe it to His secret, upholding power that what I suffered in part of this time did not rob me either of my life or senses. Yet by these sufferings the force of my evil example and inclination was lessened; I therefore have reason to count those sufferings as part of God's mercy to me.

Let me give you a very brief sketch of the geography of the circuit to which I was now confined. I may have an occasion to refer to places that I shall now mention. My trade afterwards, when the Lord allowed me to see better days, was mainly to the same places and with the same persons, where and by whom I had been considered on a level with their lowest slaves.

From Cape de Verd, the most western point of Africa, to Cape Mount the whole coast is full of rivers. The principal ones are the Gambia, Rio Grande, Sierra Leone, and Sherbro. The former is well known, and as I was never there I need say nothing. The Rio Grande, like the Nile, divides into many branches near the sea. On the most northerly, called Cacheo, the Portuguese have a settlement. The most southern branch, known by the name of Rio Nuna, is or then was the usual boundary of the white men's trade northward. Sierra Leone is a mountainous peninsula, uninhabited and inaccessible on account of the thick woods except for those parts that lie near the water.

The river is large and navigable. About twelve leagues to the southeast are three contiguous islands called the Bananas, about twenty miles in circuit. This was about the center of the white men's residence.

Seven leagues farther, the same way, lie the Plantains, three small islands about two miles distant from the continent at the point which forms one side of the Sherbro. This river is more properly a sound running within a long island and receiving the confluence of several large rivers, "rivers unknown to song," but far more deeply engraved in my remembrance than the Po or Tiber. The southernmost of these has a very peculiar course, almost parallel to the coast. It will seldom lead one more than three miles and sometimes not more than half a mile from the seashore. Indeed, it may be that all these rivers may have communications with each other and with the sea in many places.

My new master had formerly resided near Cape Mount, but now he settled at the Plantains, upon the largest of the three islands. It is a low sandy island, about two miles in circumference and almost covered with palm trees. We immediately began to build a house and to begin trading for slaves. I had now some desire to make up for lost time and to exert diligence in the tasks before me. The master was a man with whom I might have lived tolerably well if he had not been soon influenced against me. He was much under the control of a black woman who lived with him as a wife. She was a person of some importance in her own country, and he owed his initial success to her influence. The woman, I know not why, was strangely prejudiced against me from the first.[1] What made it still worse for me

51

was a severe illness that attacked me very soon after arriving before I had opportunity to show what I could or would do in his service.

Treated with Scorn and Contempt

I was sick when he sailed to Rio Nuna, and he left me in the woman's hands. At first I was taken some care of, but since I did not recover quickly, she grew weary and entirely neglected me. I sometimes had difficulty in procuring a drink of cold water when burning with a fever. My bed was a mat spread upon a board or chest, and a wood log was my pillow. When my fever left me and my appetite returned, I would gladly have eaten, but no one gave me anything. She lived in plenty herself but hardly allowed me sufficient food to sustain life. Now and then, when in the highest good humor, she would send me food from her own plate after she had dined. So greatly was my pride humbled, I received this with thanks and eagerness, as the most needy beggar receives alms.

Once, I well remember, I was called to receive this bounty from her own hand, but being exceedingly weak and feeble I dropped the plate. Those who live in plenty can hardly conceive how this loss touched me, but she had the cruelty to laugh at my disappointment. Though the table was covered with dishes (she lived mostly in the European manner), she refused to give me any more. My hunger was at times so great as to compel me to go at night and pull up roots in the plantation at the risk of being punished as a thief. These I have eaten raw upon the spot for fear of discovery. These roots are a very wholesome food, when boiled or roasted, but are as unfit to be eaten raw in any quantity much like a potato.

Sometimes strangers, even slaves in chains, helped me by secretly bringing me provisions (for they dared not be seen) from their own slender pittance.

Next to urgent hunger, nothing sits harder upon the mind than scorn and contempt. Of this I had an abundant measure. When I was very slowly recovering, this woman would sometimes pay me a visit, not to pity or relieve me but to insult me. She would call me worthless and indolent and compel me to walk, which I could hardly do. She would then send her attendants to mimic my motion, to clap their hands, laugh and throw limes at me. If they chose to throw stones, as was the case once or twice, they were not rebuked. Although all who depended on her favor had to join in this treatment, yet when she was out of sight, I was rather pitied than scorned by the lowest of her slaves.

Accused of Dishonesty

At last my master returned from his voyage. I complained of mistreatment, but he would not believe me. Since I did it in her hearing, I fared no better for it. On his second voyage, however, he took me with him. We did pretty well for a while until a fellow trader he met on the river persuaded him that I was unfaithful, that I stole his goods in the night or when he was on shore. This was almost the only vice I could not be justly charged with. The only remains of a good education I could boast of was what is commonly called honesty. As far as he had trusted me, I had been always faithful. Although my great distress might in some measure have excused it, I never once thought of defrauding him in the smallest matter. However, the charge was believed, and I was condemned without evidence.

Hunger and Exposure

From that time he likewise abused me in most cases. Whenever he left the vessel, I was locked upon deck, with a pint of rice for my day's allowance. If he stayed longer, I had no relief until his return. Indeed, I believe I would have been nearly starved but for the opportunity to catch fish sometimes. When fowls were killed for his own use, I seldom was allowed any part but the entrails to bait my hooks. At what we call slack water, that is, about the changing of the tides when the current was still, I would generally fish, and I very often succeeded. If I saw a fish upon my hook, my joy was little less than another person may have found in the success of the scheme he had most at heart. Such a fish, hastily broiled or rather half burned, without sauce, salt, or bread, has many times provided me a delicious meal.

If I caught none, I might (if I could) sleep away my hunger until the return of slack water and then try again. I also suffered from the inclemency of the weather and the lack of clothes. The rainy season was now advancing. My clothing was a shirt, a pair of trousers, a cotton handkerchief instead of a cap, and a cotton cloth, about two yards long, for upper garments. Thus dressed, I have been exposed for twenty, thirty, perhaps nearly forty hours altogether, in incessant rains accompanied with strong gales of wind and without the least shelter when my master was on shore.

I still feel some faint pangs of the violent pains I then contracted. The excessive cold and wet I endured in that voyage, and so soon after I had recovered from a long sickness, quite broke my constitution and my spirits. The latter were soon restored, but the effects of the former still remain with me as a needful memento of the service and wages of sin.

In about two months we returned. The rest of the time I remained with him was chiefly spent at the Plantains, under the same regimen as I have already mentioned. My haughty heart was now brought down, not to a wholesome repentance nor to the language of the prodigal son—this was far from me—but my spirits were sunk. I had lost all my tough determination and almost my own sense of self. Gone was the fierceness that fired me on board the *Harwich,* and that made me capable of the most desperate actions. But I was no further changed than a tiger tamed by hunger. Remove the occasion, and he will be as wild as ever.

One thing, though strange, is true. Though destitute of food and clothing, depressed to a degree beyond common wretchedness, I could sometimes concentrate my mind upon mathematical studies. I had bought Barrow's *Euclid* at Plymouth. It was the only volume I brought on shore. It was always with me, and I used to take it to remote corners of the island by the seaside and draw my diagrams with a long stick upon the sand. Thus I often beguiled my sorrows and almost forgot my feelings. Without any other assistance, I made myself, in a good measure, master of the first six books of *Euclid.*

Endnote

1. She was known as "P. I."—the phonetic spelling of her name. She was from the ruling Bombo clan who was involved in slave trading with the white traders on the coast.

6

A New Master

There is much piety and spirituality in the grateful acknowledgment of Jacob, "With my staff I passed over this Jordan, and now I am become two bands" (Gen. 32:10). These are words that seem particularly suited to my own experience. I remember some of the sad days, to which my last letter refers, when I worked at planting some lime or lemon trees. The plants I put in the ground were no taller than a young gooseberry bush. My master and his mistress, passing by the place, stopped awhile to look at me. "Who knows," said he, "who knows, but by the time these trees grow up and bear fruit, you may go home to England, obtain the command of a ship, and return to reap the fruits of your labors? We see strange things sometimes happen."

This, as he intended it, was a cutting sarcasm. I believe he thought it as probable that I should live to be king of Poland. Yet it proved to be a prediction, and one of them at least lived to see me return from England in the position he had mentioned and pluck some of the first limes from those same trees.[1] I can't proceed in my story without testifying to divine goodness by comparing my past condition with the circumstances in which the Lord has since placed me.

If you had seen me sad and alone in the dead of night, washing my one shirt upon the rocks and afterward putting it on wet so that it would dry upon my back while I slept; if you had seen my emaciated figure, so much so that when a ship's boat came to the island, my shame often forced me to hide myself in the woods from the sight of strangers; and especially if you had known that my conduct, thoughts, and feelings were still darker than my outward condition; then how impossible it would have been to imagine that a person like myself, who was so much like the apostle Paul's description— "hateful and hating one another" (Titus 3:3)—was reserved to be a special example of the providential care and overflowing goodness of God!

There was, at that time, only one sincere desire in my heart that did not go against both religion and reason. Although my sinful life made me particularly unworthy of success and although a thousand difficulties seemed to make it impossible, the Lord was pleased to grant me that one desire. But this gracious action, though great and greatly prized in itself, was a small thing compared to the blessings of His grace. He spared me to give me the knowledge of Himself, in the person of Jesus Christ. In love for my soul, He delivered me from the corruption and cast all my extreme sins behind His back. He brought my feet into the paths of peace.

When He made me acceptable to Himself in the Beloved, He gave me favor in the sight of others. He raised up new friends for me, protected and guided me through a long series of dangers, and crowned every day with repeated mercies. To Him I owe the fact that I am still alive and that I am not still living in hunger, thirst, nakedness, and destitute of all things. Into that condition I brought myself, but it was He who delivered me. He has given me a comfortable position in life, some personal knowledge of His gospel, a large number of acquaintances among His people, and friendship and correspondence with several of His most honored servants. It is as difficult to add up all my present blessings as it is to fully describe the evils and miseries of my preceding condition.

I am not sure exactly how long my miserable situation continued, but I believe it was for nearly a year. During this time I wrote two or three letters to my father. I gave him an account of my condition and asked for his assistance, suggesting at the same time that I was resolved not to return to England unless he was pleased to send for me. I also have letters that I wrote to the one I loved during that dismal period. At the lowest point, it seems, I still retained a hope of seeing her again. My father appealed to his friend in Liverpool, of whom I have spoken before. As a result, this man gave orders to one of his own captains who was then preparing to leave for Gambia and Sierra Leone.

Better Circumstances

Within the year, as I have said, my master gave his consent for me to live with another trader on the same island. Without his consent I could not be taken. He was unwilling to do it sooner, but it was then finally accomplished. This was much to my advantage: I was soon decently clothed and fed, was considered as a companion, and was given responsibility for all his household finances, totaling in cash some thousand pounds sterling.

This man had several trading stations and white servants in different places, particularly one in Kittam, along the river that nearly parallels the seacoast.[2] I was soon directed to go there, where I had a share in the management of business, jointly with another of his servants. We lived as we pleased, business flourished, and our employer was satisfied.

I began to be careless enough to think myself happy. There is a significant phrase frequently used in those parts that such a white man "has grown black." It does not refer to an alteration of one's complexion but to one's disposition. I have known several who settled in Africa after the age of thirty or forty and have at that time of life gradually grown assimilated to the personalities, customs, and ceremonies of the natives. Eventually they prefer that country to their own. They have even become dupes to all the pretended magic, necromancies, amulets, and divinations of the spiritually blind natives and put more trust in such things than even the wiser person among the natives.

A part of this spirit of infatuation was growing upon me. In time, perhaps, I might have yielded to the whole. I had closer and closer contact with the inhabitants and would have lived and died a wretch among them, if the Lord had not watched over me for good.[3] Not that I had lost those dreams that kept my heart tied to England, but my despair of ever seeing them accomplished made me willing to remain where I was. I thought I could more easily bear the disappointment in this situation than nearer home.

As soon as I had adjusted my thoughts and plans to this way of thinking, the Lord providentially interposed to break them to pieces and to save me from ruin in spite of myself.

In the meantime the ship that had orders to bring me home arrived at Sierra Leone. The captain inquired about me there and at the Banana Island but mistakenly understood that I was a great distance away in the country.[4] So he thought no more about me. Without doubt the hand of God directed my being placed at Kittam just at this time. The ship came no nearer than the Banana Island and stayed only a few days. If I had been at the Plantains, I would not perhaps have heard of her until after she had sailed. The same would certainly have happened if I had been sent to any other of my master's many trading stations. Although this place was more than a hundred miles' distance from the Plantains, I was still within a mile of the seacoast.

More remarkably, I was at that same time going in search of trade to a place some distance from the sea. I should have set out a day or two before, but we had waited for a few articles from the next ship to complete the assortment of goods I was to take with me. We sometimes walked on the beach, in expectation of seeing a vessel pass by. But this was very uncertain since at this time trade ships seldom stopped at this place. I do not know that any had stopped while I was there, although some had before when they observed a signal made from the shore.

Freed from a Captivity of Fifteen Months

In February 1747 (I don't know the exact day) my fellow servant, walking down to the beach in the afternoon, saw a vessel sailing past and made a smoke signal as a sign of our desire for trade. The ship was already a little beyond the place and since the wind was fair, the captain was uncertain whether he should stop or not. Just half an hour later and the ship would have gone beyond recall. When my companion saw her come to an anchor, he went on board from a canoe. One of the first questions he was asked was concerning me. When the captain understood I was so near, he came on shore to deliver his message.

Had an invitation from home reached me when I was sick and starving at the Plantains, I would have received it as life from the dead; but now, for the reasons already given, I reacted at first with indifference. The captain, unwilling to leave me, told a story altogether of his own imagination. He gave me a very plausible account of how he had missed a large packet of letters and papers that he should have brought with him. But he said he was sure, having heard it from my father's own mouth as well as from his employer, that a recently deceased person had left me four hundred pounds a year. He added further that if I was unable to overcome my circumstances, he had express orders to redeem me, even if it should cost one half of his cargo. Every part of this was false. I could hardly believe what he said about the estate; but since I had some expectation of an inheritance from an elderly relative, I thought a part of it might be true.

I was not long in suspense. My father's concern and desire to see me carried little weight with me and would have been insufficient to make me leave my position. The remembrance of my loved one, the hope of seeing her, and the possibility that accepting this offer might once more enable me to marry her, however, prevailed over all other considerations.

The captain further promised (and in this he kept his word) that I would be quartered in his cabin, dine at his table, and be his close companion, without his expecting any service from me. Thus I was suddenly freed from a captivity of about fifteen months. I had neither a thought of nor a desire for this change one hour before it took place. I embarked with him and in a few hours lost sight of Kittam.

God's Ruling Power and Wisdom

I was so blind and stupid at that time that I gave no thought to my good fortune nor did I seek some meaning in what had happened. Like a sea wave driven and tossed by the wind, I was controlled by my present circumstances and looked no further. But He who is eyes to the blind, was leading me in a way that I knew not.

Now that I am in some measure enlightened, I can easily perceive that it is in these seemingly fortunate circumstances that the ruling power and wisdom of God are most evidently displayed in human affairs. How many such casual events in the history of Joseph later had a necessary influence on his ensuing promotion. If he had not dreamed or if he had not told his dream; if the Midianites had passed by a day sooner or a day later; if they had sold him to any person but Potiphar; if his master's wife had been a better woman; if Pharaoh's officers had not displeased their lord; or if any or all these things had taken place in any other manner or time than they did, all that followed would have been different. The promises and purposes of God concerning Israel—her slavery, deliverance, organization, and settlement in the land—would have failed. If history had not been as it was according to God's plan, then the promised Savior, the Desire of all nations, would not have appeared. Mankind would be still in their sins, without hope, and the counsels of God's eternal love in favor of sinners defeated.

Thus we may see a connection between Joseph's first dream and the death of our Lord Christ with all its glorious consequences. So strong, though secret, is the connection between the greatest and the least important events. What a comfortable thought is this to the believer: to know that amid all the various interfering plans of men, the Lord has one constant goal, which He cannot, will not miss, namely, His own glory in the complete salvation of His people. He is wise, strong, and faithful to make even those things that seem contrary to this plan nevertheless serve to promote it.

Endnotes

1. Most likely P. I. since Newton saw her again in 1750 but no further mention is made of his master.
2. Newton uses the word "factories" to describe the slave trading posts. Slaves captured inland were sold to the slave traders who then resold the slaves to ships plying the African coast. The good location, close to an inland waterway, no doubt contributed to their flourishing business.
3. Here, as earlier, Newton doesn't explicitly say that he took an African mistress, but the implication is there. The very next sentence explains that he hadn't forgotten Mary but had given up hope of marrying her.
4. The captain was Anthony Gother, and the ship was the *Greyhound*, out of Liverpool.

7

DANGERS AND DELIVERANCES

The ship I was now on as a passenger was on a trading voyage for gold, ivory, dyers' wood, and beeswax. It requires a much longer time to collect a cargo of this sort than a cargo of slaves. The captain had begun his African trade at Gambia four or five months earlier and continued about a year after I was with him. We ranged the whole coast as far as Cape Lopez, which lies about a degree south of the equator and more than a thousand miles further from England than the place where I embarked.

I had no responsibilities to busy my thoughts, so I sometimes amused myself with mathematics. Except for this, my daily life was a course of the most terrible blasphemy and profaneness. I don't believe that I have ever since met so daring a blasphemer as myself. Not content with common profanities and cursing, I daily invented new ones so that I was often strongly rebuked by the captain who was a very passionate man and did not restrain his own temper.

A Jonah on Board

From what I told him of my past adventures and what he saw of my conduct, especially toward the close of the voyage when he met with many disasters, he would often tell me that to his grief he had a Jonah on board. A curse seemed to follow me wherever I went, and all the troubles he met with in the voyage were the result of taking me on board the vessel.

Although I was inclined to excess in almost every other outlandish behavior, I never cared for drinking. My father has often been heard to say that although I avoided drunkenness, he still entertained hopes of my recovery. But sometimes I would promote a drinking session just for the sake of a frolic, as I called it. Although I did not love the liquor, I was a slave to doing wickedness and delighted in sinfulness.

The last detestable frolic of this sort I engaged in was on the river Gabon. The instigation and expense were my own. Four or five of us sat down one evening upon deck to see who could hold out longest in drinking geneva and rum alternately.[1] A large sea shell took the place of a glass. I was very unsuited for a challenge of this sort because my head was always incapable of handling very much strong liquor. However, I proposed the first toast, which I well remember was some curse against the person who should *start* first. This proved to be me.

An Amazing Escape

My brain was soon on fire. I arose and danced about the deck like a madman. While I was thus entertaining my companions, my hat went overboard. By the light of the moon I saw the ship's boat and boldly climbed over the side to get into her so that I might recover my hat. The boat was not within my reach as I thought but was perhaps twenty feet from the ship's side. I was half over the ship's rail and in one moment more would have plunged into the water when somebody caught hold of my clothes from behind and pulled me back. This was an amazing escape since I could not swim even if I had been sober. The tide was running very strong, and my companions were too intoxicated to save me. The rest of the ship's crew was asleep. So near was I to perishing in that dreadful condition and sinking into eternity under the weight of my own curse!

Another time, at Cape Lopez, some of us had been in the woods and shot a buffalo or wild cow. We brought a part of it on board and carefully marked the place, as I thought, where we left the remainder. In the evening we returned to fetch it. I undertook to be the guide, but darkness fell before we could reach the place. We lost our way. Sometimes we were in swamps up to the middle in water. When we reached dry land, we could not tell whether we were walking toward the ship or wandering farther away. Every step increased our uncertainty. The night grew darker, and we were entangled in inextricable woods, where perhaps the foot of man had never trod before. That part of the country is entirely left to wild animals, which are found there in abundance.

We were in a terrible state, having neither light, food, nor weapons, and expecting a tiger to rush from behind every tree. The stars were clouded over, and we had no compass to tell us which way we were going. Had things continued thus, we would probably have perished; but it pleased God that no wild animal came near us. After some hours of confusion, the moon arose and pointed out the easterly direction. It was clear then, as we had expected, that instead of drawing nearer to the seaside, we had been moving toward the interior. By the guidance of the moon, we finally came to the shore a considerable distance from the ship. We got safe on board without any further inconvenience than what we suffered from fear and fatigue.

These and many other deliverances were all at that time entirely lost upon me. The warnings of my conscience had grown weaker and weaker with my refusals to pay attention and at last entirely ceased. For a period of many months, if not for some years, I cannot recall that I was restrained by my conscience. At times I was seriously ill and believe that I was near death, but I did not have the least concern about the consequences. I seemed to have every mark of a complete lack of repentance and rejection of God. Neither God's judgments nor mercies made the least impression on me.

Sails for Home

Our business being finished, we left Cape Lopez, and stayed a few days at the island of Annobon to lay in provisions. We sailed homeward about the beginning of January 1748. From Annobon to England, without touching at any intermediate port, is a very long navigation—perhaps more than seven thousand miles if we include the route necessary on account of the trade winds.

We sailed first westward, until near the coast of Brazil, then northward to the banks of Newfoundland. There were the usual variations of wind and weather, but without meeting anything extraordinary. On these banks we stopped half a day to fish for cod. This was mainly done for some diversion. We had provisions enough and hardly expected those fish to be all we would have to subsist on. We left the banks March 1 with a hard westerly wind that pushed us homeward quickly. Because of the length of the voyage in a hot climate, the vessel greatly needed repair and was unfit for stormy weather. The sails and robes were worn, and many circumstances concurred to render what followed all the more dangerous.[2]

On March 9, the day before our catastrophe, I unthinkingly took up Stanhope's Thomas à Kempis, as I had often done before, to pass away the time.[3] I read it with indifference as if it were entirely a romance. However, while I was reading this time, an involuntary suggestion arose in my mind: What if these things were true? I could not bear the force of the inference as it related to myself; therefore I shut the book quickly. My conscience accused me once more, and I concluded that, true or false, I must take the consequences of my own choices. I put an abrupt end to these reflections by joining in with some idle conversation that came along.

The Lord's Time

But now the Lord's time was come, and the conviction I was so unwilling to receive was deeply impressed upon me. I went to bed that night in my usual self-confidence and indifference, but I was awakened from a sound sleep by the force of a violent sea that broke over the ship. It flooded below decks and filled the cabin where I slept with water. This alarming development was followed by a cry from the deck that the ship was going down or sinking. As soon as I could gather my wits, I started to go up on deck, but was met on the ladder by the captain, who ordered me to bring a knife with me.

While I returned for the knife, another person went up in my place and was quickly washed overboard. We had no time to mourn him nor did we expect to survive him for very long for we soon found that the ship was filling up with water very quickly. The sea had torn away the upper timbers on one side and made the ship a mere wreck in a few minutes.[4]

Considering the circumstances, it was astonishing and almost miraculous that any of us survived. We immediately manned the pumps, but the water increased against all our efforts. Some of us went to work bailing in another part of the vessel, scooping the water out with buckets and pails. We had only eleven or twelve people for this job. In spite of all we could do, she was full of water or very near it. With a common cargo she would have sunk, of course, but we had a great quantity of beeswax and wood on board, which were specifically lighter than the water. As God allowed, we suffered this damage at the very height of the gale; but toward morning we were able to employ some measures for our safety that succeeded beyond hope.

In about an hour's time the day began to break and the wind abated. We used most of our clothes and bedding to stop the leaks, although the weather was exceedingly cold, especially since we had so lately left a hot climate. Over these we nailed pieces of boards, and at last saw the water abate. At the beginning of this I was little affected. I pumped hard and tried to encourage myself and my companions. I told one of them that in a few days this distress would be our topic of conversation over a glass of wine; but he, being a less hardened sinner than myself, replied with tears, "No, it is too late now."

About nine o'clock, being almost exhausted from the cold and work, I went to speak with the captain, who was busy elsewhere.

As I was returning, I said, almost without any meaning, "If this doesn't work, the Lord have mercy on us!" This (though spoken with little reflection) was the first desire I had breathed for mercy for many years. I was instantly struck with my own words. What mercy can there be for me? I had to return to the pump, and there I continued *until noon.*

Almost every passing wave broke over my head, but we tied ourselves fast with ropes so that we wouldn't be washed away. Indeed, I expected that every time the vessel descended into the trough of the waves, she would not rise again. I dreaded the possibility of death now. My heart feared the worst if the Scriptures, which I had long since opposed, were true. Still I was but half convinced and remained for a space of time in an irritable frame, a mixture of despair and impatience. I thought that if the Christian religion were true, I could not be forgiven. I was therefore expecting, and almost at times wishing, to know the worst.

Endnotes

1. Geneva was distilled alcohol flavored with juniper berries. It later became the common term for gin, the cheap drink of the poor that wreaked social havoc in England in the early 1700s. So pervasive were its effects and so ineffective were the attempted remedies that it has been compared to the drug culture of the latter twentieth century (see Patrick Dillon, *Gin: The Much Lamented Death of Madam Geneva,* Justin, Charles, & Co., 2003). John Wesley and the Methodist church that arose in the latter 1700s strongly opposed the use of alcohol due to the social degradation resulting from gin use.
2. Trading ships in general and slave ships in particular, with lower decks designed to cram as many slaves as possible into the ship, were built at minimum expense in order to maximize profits.

3. An edition of the classic work *On the Imitation of Christ*, first published in 1418 and still read not only during Newton's time but into the modern era as well.
4. Newton adds, "I shall not describe the disaster in the marine dialect, which would be understood by few; therefore I can give you but a very inadequate idea of it."

8

VOYAGE HOMEWARD

March 21 is a day for me to remember. I have never allowed it to pass completely unnoticed since 1748. On that day the Lord of heaven delivered me out of deep waters.

I continued at the pump from three in the morning until near noon, and then I could do no more. I went and lay down upon my bed, uncertain and almost uncaring as to whether I should rise again. In an hour's time I was called. Not being able to pump, I went to the helm and steered the ship until midnight, expecting a short relief break.

Here I had time to think of my former religious professions, of the divine calls, warnings, and deliverances I had met with. I thought of the licentious course of my life, particularly my unparalleled audacity in making the gospel the subject of profane ridicule. I thought that surely the Scripture proved that there never was, nor could be, such a sinner as myself. Then, considering the advantages I had disregarded, I concluded at first that my sins were too great to be forgiven.

The Scriptures seemed to say the same. Before this I was well acquainted with the Bible. Many passages returned to my memory on this occasion, particularly those fearful passages that speak of

I went to the helm, and steered the ship until midnight.

the judgment of those who know the way of truth but turn from it.[1] They seemed so exactly to suit my situation and character that they were obvious proof of a divine origin. Thus, as I have said, I waited with fear and impatience to receive my inevitable doom.

Even though I had thoughts of this kind, they were exceedingly weak and unformed. It was not until several years, when I had gained some clearer understanding of the infinite righteousness and grace of Jesus Christ my Lord, that I had a deep and solid understanding of my condition by nature and practice. Perhaps until then I could not have borne the sight, so wonderfully does the Lord proportion the discoveries of sin and grace. He knows our human nature; if He were to demonstrate all at once the greatness of His power, a poor sinner would be instantly overwhelmed and crushed like a moth.

The Exercises of His Mind

When I saw beyond all probability that there was still hope of relief and heard about six in the evening that the ship was free of water, there arose a gleam of hope. I thought I saw the hand of God displayed in our favor, and I began to pray. I could not utter the prayer of faith. I could not draw near to a reconciled God and call Him Father. My prayer was like the cry of ravens, which yet the Lord does not disdain to hear. I now began to think of that Jesus whom I had so often derided. I recollected the particulars of His life and of His death—a death for sins not His own, but for those who in their distress should put their trust in Him. And now I mainly wanted evidence. The comfortless principles of unbelief were deeply riveted within me, and I wished, rather than believed, that these things were real facts.

The great question now for me was how to obtain faith. I do not mean an appropriating faith, of which I then knew neither the nature nor necessity. Rather I wished to gain assurance that the Scriptures were of divine inspiration and a sufficient reason to exercise trust and hope in God. One of the first helps I received, as a result of my determination to examine the New Testament more carefully, was from Luke 11:13. I understood that to profess faith in Jesus Christ, when in reality I did not believe His history, was no better than a mockery of the heart-searching God. Here, however, I found a Spirit spoken of, which was to be given to those who ask for it. I reasoned thus: if this book is true, the promise in this passage is true likewise. I need that very Spirit by which the whole was written, in order to understand it. He has promised here to give that Spirit to those who ask. I must therefore pray, and if it is of God, He will make good His own word. My purposes were strengthened by John 7:17. I concluded that, although I could not say from my heart that I believed the gospel, yet I would for the present take it for granted. By studying it in this light, I would be more and more confirmed in it.

If what I am writing is read by our modern atheists, they would say (for I know their thinking) that I wanted to persuade myself of this opinion. I confess that I did. So would they, if the Lord showed them, as He was pleased to show me at that time, the absolute necessity of some means of reconciliation to come between a righteous God and a sinful soul. In the gospel I saw at least a chance of hope, but on every other side I was surrounded with black, unfathomable despair.

The wind was now moderate, but continued fair, and we were drawing nearer to our port. We began to recover from our consternation, although we were greatly alarmed by our circumstances. The water had floated all our containers in the hold. All the wooden casks of supplies had been beaten to pieces by the violent motion of the ship. Our livestock, such as pigs, sheep, and poultry, had been washed overboard in the storm.

We saved all the provisions, except the fish I mentioned previously, and some food intended for the hogs (there was only a little of this left). This would have fed us for only a week at scanty rations. The sails, too, were mostly blown away so that we advanced slowly even when the wind was fairly strong. We imagined ourselves about a hundred leagues from the land, but were in reality much farther. Thus we proceeded, alternating between hope and fear. My spare time was chiefly employed in reading and meditating on the Scriptures and praying to the Lord for mercy and instruction.

Disappointments

Things continued thus for four or five days, perhaps longer. We were awakened one morning by the joyful shouts of the look-outs upon deck, proclaiming the sight of land. The dawning was uncommonly beautiful. The light, just strong enough to show distant objects, presented us with a heart-lifting scene. It seemed there was a mountainous coast, about twenty miles from us, terminating in a cape or point. A little farther, two or three small islands seemed to be rising out of the water. Their appearance and position seemed exactly the answer to our hopes, resembling the northwest extremity of Ireland, which we were steering for. We congratulated each other, having no doubt that if the wind continued, we would be safe and well-supplied the next day.

The remainder of our brandy (a little more than a pint) was, by the captain's orders, distributed among us. We also ate up the remainder of our bread, overjoyed at this welcome sight. We were like men suddenly reprieved from death. While we were in high spirits, the mate, with a graver tone than the rest, sunk our spirits by saying that he hoped it might turn out to be land at last. If one of the common sailors had first said this, the rest would have beaten him for raising such an unreasonable doubt.

It brought on, however, heated debates and disputes as to whether or not it was land. The case was soon unanswerably decided. The dawn was advancing quickly, and in a little while one of our fancied islands began to grow red from the approach of the sun, which soon arose just under it. We had squandered our bread too hastily. Our land was nothing but clouds. In half an hour more the whole appearance of land dissolved.

Seamen have often known deceptions of this sort, but in our distress we were unwilling to be undeceived. We comforted ourselves, however, with the thought that though we could not see the land yet, we should soon—if wind continued fair. But alas! We were deprived of this hope also. That same day our favorable wind subsided, and the next morning a storm sprung up from the southwest. It came directly against us and continued for more than two weeks. The ship was so wrecked that we were obliged to keep the wind always on the broken side, unless the weather was quite moderate. With the wind in that quarter, we were driven still farther from our port toward the northward of all Ireland. We were headed as far as the Lewis or western islands of Scotland, but a long way to the west. As a result, our position deprived us of any hope of being relieved by other vessels. Indeed, we may even have been the very first ship to be in that part of the ocean at that season of the year.

Provisions now began to grow very short. Half of a salted cod was a day's food for twelve people. We had plenty of fresh water, but not a drop of liquor, no bread, hardly any clothes, and very cold weather. We had to constantly man the pumps to keep the ship above water. Relentless work with little food wore us down quickly, and one man died. Our sufferings, however, were light in comparison to our fears. We had the terrible prospect of either being starved to death or reduced to eat one another. Our expectations grew more depressed every day, and I had a further problem peculiar to myself.

The captain, whose temperament was quite soured by distress, was repeatedly blaming me as the sole cause of the calamity. He was confident that if I was thrown overboard, as their only recourse, they would be preserved from death. He did not intend to commit the deed, but the continual repetition of this gave me much distress, especially as my conscience seconded his words. I thought it very probable that all that had happened to us was my fault.

The powerful hand of God had at last found me out.

As we proceeded, however, I began to feel a hope greater than all my fears. Just when we were ready to give up all for lost and despair was on every face, the wind came about to the very direction we wished for. This direction was best suited for keeping the broken part of the ship out of the water. As gently as our few remaining sails could bear, the wind continued (although it was a stormy time of the year) until we once more were called on deck to see land.

We saw the island Tory, and the next day we anchored in Lough

Swilly, Ireland. This was April 8, just four weeks after the damage we sustained from the storm. When we came into this port, our very last provisions were boiling in the pot. Before we had been there for even two hours, the wind began to blow with great force. If we had continued at sea that night in our shattered, enfeebled condition, we would more than likely have gone to the bottom. About this time I began to know that there is a God who hears and answers prayer. How many times has He answered me since this great deliverance! Yet, alas! How distrustful and ungrateful is my heart even until the present!

Endnote

1. Newton mentions specifically Proverbs 1:24–31; Hebrews 6:4–6; and 2 Peter 2:20.

9

RELIGIOUS AWAKENINGS

Before proceeding, I will look back a little and give you some further account of the state of my mind. The predicaments of hunger, cold, and weariness, and the fears of sinking and starving I shared in common with others. But besides these I felt a heart-bitterness that was completely my own. No one else on board was impressed with any sense of the hand of God in our danger and deliverance.

No earthly incidents of God's providence can reach the heart unless the Lord Himself applies them. My companions were either quite unaffected by the danger or soon forgot; but it was not so with me. I was not any wiser or better than they were, but the Lord was pleased to bestow upon me a special mercy. I was the most unlikely person in the ship to receive an impression upon my conscience, having been often before quite stupid and hard-hearted in the very face of great dangers. I had always before been more and more stubborn after every reproof. I can see no reason why the Lord singled me out for mercy but "that so it seemed good to Him" (1 Sam. 3:18) and to show by one astonishing instance that "with Him nothing is impossible" (Luke 1:37).

Becomes More Serious and Earnest

There was no one on board to whom I could speak freely concerning the state of my soul, none to ask for advice. As for books, I had a New Testament, Stanhope, and a volume of Bishop Beveridge's sermons (one on our Lord's Passion affected me greatly).[1] In reading through the New Testament, I was struck with several passages: the fig tree (Luke 13); the case of St. Paul (1 Tim. 1); but particularly the prodigal son (Luke 15). I thought that I must be the very best example of the prodigal. The goodness of the father in receiving, even in running to meet such a son, became clearer to me as an illustration of the Lord's goodness to returning sinners.

I continued to pray regularly. The Lord had intervened so far to save me, and I hoped He would continue to act. Outward circumstances helped to make me still more serious and sincere in crying out to Him who alone could relieve me. Sometimes I thought I would be happy to starve to death if I could die as a believer. To this point my prayers had been answered in that even before we arrived in Ireland I had satisfactory evidence in my own mind as to the truth of the gospel and its exact suitability for all my needs. I saw that God could declare not only His mercy but also His justice in the pardon of sins on account of the obedience and sufferings of Jesus Christ. By that time I had embraced the inspiring doctrine of "God manifest in the flesh, reconciling the world to Himself" (2 Cor. 5:19).

I had no idea of other religious systems that allowed the Savior no higher honor than that of an upper servant or, at most, a demigod. I was in need of an Almighty Savior, and such was the one I found described in the New Testament. The Lord had worked a marvelous thing: I was no longer an atheist. I heartily renounced my former profaneness. I was sincerely touched with a sense of undeserved mercy in being brought safe through so many dangers. I was sorry for my past misspent life and committed myself to an immediate reformation. I was freed from the habit of swearing, which seemed to have been as deeply rooted in me as a second nature. To all appearances, I was a new man.

Depending on His Own Will

I do not doubt that this change, so far as it lasted, was brought about by the Spirit and power of God; yet I was greatly deficient in many respects. On one hand, I was aware of my more enormous sins, but on the other I was hardly aware of the innate evils of my heart. I had no comprehension of the spirituality and extent of the law of God. The hidden life of a Christian— communion with God by Jesus Christ and dependence on Him for hourly supplies of wisdom, strength, and comfort—was a mystery of which I had no understanding. I acknowledged the Lord's mercy in pardoning what was past, but I depended chiefly upon my own resolution to do better for the future.

I had no Christian friend or faithful minister to advise me that my strength was no more than my own self-righteousness. I began to look for serious books, but having no spiritual discernment, I frequently made a wrong choice. I was not exposed to evangelical preaching or conversation, except for a few times. Even then I heard but did not understand, not until six years later. These things the Lord was pleased to show me gradually. I learned them here a little and there a little, by painful experience.

The teaching wasn't done by ordinary means and took place among the same evil company and bad examples I had known for some time.

After this period I could no longer make a mockery of sin or a joke of holy things. I no longer questioned the truth of Scripture or quenched the rebukes of conscience. I consider this as the beginning of my return to God or rather of His return to me. I cannot consider myself to have been a believer in the full sense of the word, however, until a considerable time later.

I related that in the time of our distress we had plenty of fresh water. This was a considerable relief to us, especially since our diet was mostly salted fish without bread. We drank plentifully and were not afraid of lacking water, yet our supply was much nearer the end than we expected. We thought that we had six large barrels of water on board. It was good that we were safe in Ireland before we discovered that five of them were empty. They had been moved out of their places by the violent motions of the ship when it was full of water. If we had found this out while still at sea, it would have greatly increased our distress since we would have drunk more sparingly.[2]

In Ireland: A Serious Professor

While the ship was refitted at Lough Swilly, I returned to Londonderry. I lodged at a very good house where I was treated with much kindness and soon recovered my health and strength. Twice a day I went to the prayers at church and determined to receive the sacrament at the next opportunity. Finally the day came. I got up very early, was very earnest in my private devotions, and, with the greatest solemnity committed myself to be the Lord's forever and only His. This was not a formal ritual, but was still a sincere surrender of myself, conscious of the mercies I had so recently received. Lacking a better knowledge of myself and of the subtlety of Satan's temptations, I was later seduced to forget these vows. However, though my views of the gospel of salvation were very vague, I experienced a peace and satisfaction in the sacraments that day which were entirely new to me.

The next day I went shooting with the mayor of the city and some other gentlemen. As I climbed up a steep bank, pulling my shotgun after me in a perpendicular direction, it went off so near my face that it burned away the corner of my hat. Thus even when we think we are safe, we are no less exposed to danger than when all seems conspiring to destroy us. The divine providence which is sufficient to deliver us in our utmost distress is equally necessary in the most peaceful situation.

During our stay in Ireland, I wrote home. The vessel I was in had not been heard of for eighteen months and had been given up for lost long before. My father did not expect to hear that I was alive, but he received my letter a few days before he left London. He was just leaving to become governor of York Fort, in Hudson's Bay, and he never returned. He sailed before I landed in England. He had planned to take me with him but, God designing otherwise, one hindrance or another delayed us in Ireland until it was too late. I received two or three affectionate letters from him, but I never had the pleasure of seeing him again. I hoped that three years later I would have an opportunity to ask his forgiveness for the anxiety my disobedience had caused him; but the ship that was to have brought him home arrived without him.

Before his departure, my father paid a visit to my friends in

Kent and gave his consent to the union that had been so long talked of. When I returned, therefore, I found I had only to obtain the consent of one person. With her, I stood at as great an uncertainty as the first day I saw her.

Restoration of Some Measure

I arrived at Liverpool the end of May 1748, about the same day that my father sailed; but the Lord had found me another father in the gentleman whose ship had brought me home.[3] He received me with great tenderness and the most sincere promises of friendship and assistance, which he has since kept. To him, as the instrument of God's goodness, I owe my all. Yet even this friend could not have saved me effectually if the Lord had not met with me on my way home. Until then I was like the man possessed of the legion of demons. No arguments, no persuasion, no remembrance of the past, or regard to the future could have restrained me within the bounds of common sense. But now I was, in some measure, restored to my senses.

My friend immediately offered me the command of a ship, but after mature consideration, I declined for the present. Since I had been unsettled and careless before, I thought it best to make another voyage first, learn to obey, and acquire further insight and experience in business before I undertook such a responsibility.

The mate of the vessel I came home in was given the command of a new ship, and I signed on as mate to him.[4] I made a short visit to London but had only one opportunity of seeing the one I loved. I always was very awkward in pleading my own cause in our conversation. After my return to Liverpool, I put the question of marriage in such a manner by letter that she could not avoid coming to some sort of decision. Her answer, though cautious, satisfied me. I understood from it that she was free from any other engagement and was willing to wait until after the voyage I had undertaken.

Endnotes

1. William Beveridge (1637–1708), bishop of St. Asaph. Several of his religious works were published after his death.
2. The combination of salted food with scarce water rations would have created a maddening thirst.
3. Joseph Manesty, who had tried to help the younger Newton out of difficulty before.
4. Richard Jackson, mate on the *Greyhound*, was now captain of the *Brownlow*.

10

ADVENTURES AS A SLAVE DEALER

Imagine a number of ships, at different times and from different places, heading for the same port. There are some things in which all would agree—the compass direction to steer by, the destination, the general rules of navigation—these would be the same for all. In other respects they would differ. Perhaps no two of them would meet with the same distribution of winds and weather. Some would set out with a favorable wind, but when they almost think their passage secure, they are checked by adverse winds. After enduring much hardship, danger, and frequent expectations of shipwreck, they barely escape and reach the desired haven.

Others meet the greatest difficulties at first. They set forth in a storm and are often beaten back. At length their voyage proves favorable and they enter the port with a rich and abundant success. Some are attacked by privateers and enemies and obliged to fight their way through. Others meet with few remarkable events in their passage.

The Experiences of Believers

Is it not the same in the spiritual life? All true believers walk by the same rule and mind the same things. The Word of God is their compass, Jesus is both their polar star and their sun of righteousness, and their hearts and their faces are all set Zion-ward. They are as one body, animated by one spirit; yet their experiences, formed upon these common principles, are far from being uniform. The Lord in His first call, and His following providential actions, regards the situation, temperament, and talents of each and the particular services or trials He has appointed for them. All are tested at times yet some pass through the voyage of life much more smoothly than others. But He "who walketh upon the wings of the wind" (Ps. 104:3) and "measures the water in the hollow of His hand" (Isa. 40:12) will not suffer any in His charge to perish in the storms, although for a season, perhaps, many of them are ready to give up hope.

We must not, therefore, make the experience of others, in all respects, a rule to ourselves nor our own a rule to others. These are common mistakes that spawn other mistakes as well. My case has been extraordinary. I have hardly met another case resembling it. Only a very few have been recovered from such a dreadful state. The few that have been thus favored have generally passed through the most severe convictions. After the Lord has given them peace, their future lives have been usually more zealous, bright, and exemplary than is common.

On the one hand, my convictions were very moderate and far below what might have been expected. On the other hand, my first beginnings in a religious path were as faint as can be imagined. I never knew that season alluded to in Scripture usually called the time of the first love (Jer. 2:2; Rev. 2:4). It is to be expected that after such a wonderful, unhoped for deliverance as I had received and after my eyes were somewhat enlightened to see things aright, I should immediately cleave to the Lord and His ways with purpose of heart and depend no more on mere flesh and blood.

Alas! It was quite the opposite with me. I had learned to pray. I set some value upon the Word of God and was no longer a libertine, but my soul still cleaved to the dust. Soon after my departure from Liverpool, I began to grow slack in waiting upon the Lord. I fell into trivial conversation. Though my heart rebuked me often, my armor was gone, and I declined quickly. By the time I arrived at Guinea, I seemed to have forgotten all the Lord's mercies. Profaneness excepted, I was almost as bad as before. The enemy prepared a train of temptations, and I became his easy prey. For about a month, he lulled me asleep in a course of evil, of which a few months before, I could not have supposed myself any longer capable.

The Deceitfulness of Sin

"Take heed, lest any of you be hardened through the deceitfulness of sin!" (Heb. 3:13). Sin first deceives, and then it hardens. I was now fast bound in chains; I had little desire and no power at all to free myself. I would at times reflect on my condition, but if I attempted to struggle, it was in vain. I was just like Samson, when he said, "I will go forth, and shake myself, as at other times" (Judg. 16:20), but the Lord was departed and he was helpless in the hands of his enemies. In recalling this period, the Lord has often reminded me what a poor creature I am in myself, incapable of standing a single hour without continual, fresh supplies of strength and grace from the fountainhead.

At length the Lord, whose mercies are infinite, intervened on my behalf. My business in this voyage, while along the coast, was to sail from place to place in the longboat to purchase slaves. The ship was at Sierra Leone, and I was then at the Plantains, the scene of my former captivity. I was in comfortable circumstances, courted by those who had formerly despised me. The lime trees I had planted were growing tall. They promised fruit the following year, at which time I expected to return with a ship of my own.

Sick with a Violent Fever

But none of these things affected me, until the Lord again intervened to save me. He visited me with a violent fever, which broke the fatal chain and once more brought me to myself. But oh, what an experience! My past dangers and deliverances, my earnest prayers in the time of trouble, my solemn vows before the Lord at His table, and my ungrateful returns for all His goodness were all brought to my mind at once. I began to wish that the Lord had allowed me to sink into the ocean when I first sought His mercy. For a little while I concluded that the door of hope was shut, but this continued for only a short while. Weak and almost delirious, I arose from my bed and crept to a secluded part of the island. There I found a renewed liberty to pray. I made no more resolutions but cast myself before the Lord to do with me as He should please. I do not remember that any particular text or remarkable discovery was presented to my mind; but, in general, I was enabled to hope and believe in a crucified Savior.

The burden was removed from my conscience, and not only

my peace but my health was restored. I cannot say it was instantaneous, but I began to recover from that hour. When I returned to the ship, two days afterward, I was perfectly well before I got on board. From that time since I trust I have been delivered from the power and dominion of sin. As to the effects and conflicts of sin dwelling in me, I still "groan, being burdened" (2 Cor. 5:4).

I now began again to wait upon the Lord. I have often grieved His Spirit and foolishly wandered from Him since (when, alas! shall I be more wise?). His powerful grace, however, has preserved me from such black declines as I have just recorded. I humbly trust in His mercy and promises that He will be my guide and guard to the end.

My leisure hours in this voyage were chiefly employed in learning Latin, which I had now entirely forgot. This desire was sparked by seeing one of Horace's lyric poems in a magazine.[1] By concerted effort, often waking when I might have slept, I made some progress before I returned. I not only understood the sense and meaning of many poems and some of the epistles but also began to relish the beauties of the composition and acquired a spice of what Mr. Law calls "classical enthusiasm." Indeed, I had Horace more in my mind than some who are masters of the Latin language. My resources were so few that I generally had the passage fixed in my memory before I could fully understand its meaning.

During the eight months we were on the coast, I was exposed to innumerable dangers and perils: from the burning sun and chilling dews; from winds and thunderstorms; in the open boat and on shore; from long journeys through the woods; and the disposition of the natives who are in many places cruel, treacherous, and watching for opportunities for mischief. Several boats in that time were cut off, and several white men poisoned. In my own boat I buried six or seven people with fevers. When going on shore or returning in the little canoes, I have been more than once or twice overturned by the violence of the surf or ocean waves. I was brought to land half dead for I could not swim. An account of the escapes I still remember would swell to several pages; many more I have perhaps forgotten. I shall select only one instance as a specimen of that wonderful providence that watched over me.

A Providential Escape

When our trade was finished and we were near sailing to the West Indies, the only remaining service I had to perform in the boat was to assist in bringing the wood and water from the shore. We were then at Rio Cestors. I used to go up the river in the afternoon with the sea breeze, procure my cargo in the evening, and return on board in the morning with the land wind. Several of these little voyages I had made, but the boat was old and almost unfit for use.

One day, having dined on board, I was preparing to return to the river. As usual, I had taken leave of the captain, received his orders, was ready in the boat, and just going to let go of our ropes and sail from the ship. In that instant the captain came up from the cabin and called me on board again. I went, expecting further orders, but he said that I should remain that day in the ship and ordered another man to go in my place. I was surprised at this since the boat had never been sent away without me before. I asked him the reason, but he could give me no reason but that is as he would have it.

Accordingly, the boat went without me and never returned. She sank that night in the river, and the person who had taken my place was drowned. I was greatly affected when we received news of the event the next morning. The captain himself, a stranger to religion, could not help being affected. He declared that he had no other reason for countermanding me at that time, but that it came suddenly into his mind to detain me.

Endnote

1. Horace, the Roman poet, lived 65–8 B.C.

11

Marriage and Command of a Ship

A few days after I was thus wonderfully saved from unforeseen danger, we sailed for Antigua and from there proceeded to Charlestown, South Carolina.[1] In this place were many sincere Christians, but I didn't know where to find them. Indeed, I wasn't aware of a difference, but assumed that all who attended public worship were good Christians. I was just as in the dark about preaching, thinking that whatever came from the pulpit must be true. I had two or three opportunities to hear a dissenting minister named Smith. By what I have known since, I believe that he was an excellent and powerful preacher of the gospel. There was something in his manner that impressed me, but I did not completely understand him. The best words that men can speak are ineffectual until explained and applied by the Spirit of God. He alone can open the heart. It pleased the Lord that for some time I did not learn more than what He enabled me to collect from my own experience and reflection.

My conduct was now very inconsistent. Almost every day, when business would permit, I used to retire into the woods and fields. I trust I began to taste the sweets of communion with God in prayer and praise. Yet I frequently spent the evenings with worthless company. My relish for worldly diversions was considerably weakened, and I was more of a spectator than a sharer in their pleasures; but I did not as yet see the necessity of separation. Since my conformity with old habits and companions was chiefly due to lack of understanding, rather than to an obstinate attachment, the Lord was pleased to preserve me from what I *knew* was sinful. I had, for the most part, peace of conscience, and my strongest desires were toward the things of God.

Not understanding the power of that precept, "Abstain from all appearance of evil" (1 Thess. 5:22), I very often went to the brink of temptation; yet the Lord was gracious to my weakness and did not allow the enemy to prevail against me. I was gradually led to see the unseemliness and folly of one thing after another. When I saw it, the Lord strengthened me to give it up. But it was some years before I was delivered from occasional practice of many things that at this time I do not allow myself.

We finished our voyage and arrived in Liverpool. When the ship's affairs were settled, I went to London and from there, as you may guess, to Kent. More than seven years had passed since my first visit. Through the overruling goodness of God, while I seemed abandoned to myself and blindly following my own headstrong passions, I was guided to the accomplishment of my one desire. Every obstacle was now removed. I had renounced my former follies, and my occupation was established. With friends on all sides consenting, the question was now entirely between ourselves. Accordingly our hands were joined in marriage on February 1, 1750.

The satisfaction I have found in this union was greatly heightened by reflection on the past difficulties I had passed through and the extraordinary mercy and providence of the Lord in bringing it to pass. Considering my time as a virtual slave under my first master, it seems that few persons have known more either of the misery or happiness of which human life is capable.

At age seventeen I was still immature in judgment, and my affections might have been set upon someone without any hope of fulfillment or with severe disappointment! The long delay was a mercy. Had I married a year or two sooner, before the Lord was pleased to change my heart, we would have been mutually unhappy even unto the present. "Surely mercy and goodness have followed me all my days" (Ps. 23:6).

Resting in the Gift and Forgetting the Giver

But, alas! I soon began to feel that my heart was still hard and ungrateful to the God of my life. This crowning mercy, which gave me all I could ask for or wish in terms of earthly success and which ought to have resulted in obedience and praise, had a contrary effect. I rested in the gift and forgot the Giver. My poor small heart was satisfied. A cold and neglectful frame of mind concerning spiritual things developed and gained ground daily. Happily for me, in June I received orders to return to Liverpool. This roused me from my forgetfulness. Naturally I found the pains of absence and separation as great as my preceding pleasure. It was hard, very hard, to part especially since my conscience suggested that I hardly deserved that we should be spared to meet again.

But the Lord supported me. I was a poor, faint, idolatrous being, but I now had some experience of the way of access to the throne of grace by the blood of Jesus, and peace was soon restored. Yet through the entire following voyage, my irregular and excessive emotions were as thorns in my eyes. They often made my other blessings seem tasteless and dull. But He who does all things well overruled this also for my good. It gave me renewed purpose in prayer, both for my wife and myself; it increased my unconcern for company and amusement. It made me accustomed to a kind of voluntary self-denial, which I later learned to improve for even a better purpose.

While I remained in England, we corresponded regularly by letter. While I was at sea, I constantly kept up the practice of writing two or three times a week, if weather and business permitted (although there was no way to convey my letters homeward for six or eight months at a time). Since not one of my letters was lost, I have nearly two hundred pages now lying in my desk of that correspondence.

This diversion, by which I hoped to soften the period of absence, had a good effect beyond my main intention. It caused me to think and write upon a wide variety of subjects, and I acquired a greater skill in expressing myself than I would otherwise have attained. As I gained more ground in religious knowledge, my letters became more serious. At times, I still find it advantageous to look them over. They especially remind me of many providential incidents and the state of my mind at different periods during those voyages, which would otherwise have escaped my memory.

I sailed from Liverpool in August 1750 as commander of a good ship. Having now the command and care of thirty persons, I endeavored to treat them humanely and to give them a good example. I established public worship, according to the liturgy, twice every Lord's day and officiated myself. I did not go further than this while I continued in that employment.[2]

Having now much leisure time, I committed myself to the study of Latin with good success. In the space of two or three voyages I became tolerably acquainted with the best classics.[3] I conceived a plan of becoming a Ciceronian myself, and I thought it would be a fine thing indeed to write pure and elegant Latin. I wrote some essays, but by this time the Lord was pleased to draw me nearer to Himself. He gave me a fuller view of the "Pearl of great price" (Matt. 13:46), the inestimable treasure hid in the field of the Holy Scriptures. For the sake of this, I was willing to part with all my newly-acquired riches.

I began to think that life was too short, especially my life, for such elaborate trifling. Neither poet nor historian could tell me a word of Jesus, and I therefore applied myself to those who could. The classics were at first confined to one morning in the week, and at length completely laid aside. I prefer Buchanan's Psalms to a whole shelf of Elzevirs.[4] I have gained much from Latin since it enables me to read any useful or interesting book in that language. Beyond this, however, I have no interest. About the same time, and for the same reason, I laid aside mathematics. I found that it not only took up considerable time, but also so engrossed my thoughts that my head was literally full of it. I was weary of cold contemplative truths that can neither warm nor amend the heart, but rather tend to amplify self. I found no traces of this "wisdom" in the life of Jesus or the writings of Paul. I do not regret that I have had some opportunities of knowing the first principles of these things, but I praise the Lord that He inclined me to stop in time. While I was "spending my labor for that which is not bread" (Isa. 55:2), He was pleased to set before me "wine and milk, without money and without price" (Isa. 55:1).

My first voyage was fourteen months and occasioned some danger and difficulties but nothing very remarkable.[5] As I intend to be more specific concerning the second voyage, I will only say that I was preserved from every harm. Having seen many fall on my right hand and on my left, I was brought home in peace and returned on November 2, 1751, to the place that was often in my thoughts.

Endnotes

1. The *Brownlow* left Africa with 218 slaves but over 60 died in the ocean crossing, known as the "middle passage."
2. Newton doesn't mention here that his father drowned in June, 1750, while swimming and was buried at Fort York in Hudson Bay.
3. "I read Terence, Virgil, several pieces of Cicero, and the modern classics, Buchanan, Erasmus, and Cassimir." George Buchanan (1506–1582) was a Scottish historian and scholar.
4. The Elzevir family were celebrated Dutch printers, whose first printed editions date to 1592. Newton is probably referring to the Elzevir series of classical Latin, French, and Italian authors released in the 1600s.
5. Missing from Newton's growing spiritual consciousness is an awareness of the intrinsic evil of his own occupation—slave trading. Steve Turner observes:

> Like almost everyone of his generation he saw nothing inherently wrong with slavery and therefore no inconsistency in participating in it as a follower of Jesus. Of all the Christian denominations only the Quakers and Anabaptists had denounced slavery. Powerful traders belonged to the church—Joseph Manesty owned half a pew at St. George's Church in Derby Square, Liverpool—and some Christians argued passionately that slavery was God's way of rescuing Africans from their barbaric practices and heathen beliefs and introducing them to Christianity. Using this perspective, slavery could easily be harmonized with Christianity. The only improvements a Christian trader might make would be to treat the slaves more compassionately (*Amazing Grace, The Story of America's Most Beloved Song*, p. 50).

Years of further spiritual growth would lead Newton to a new awareness of slavery as a moral evil. He became the spiritual mentor of William Wilberforce, who led the antislavery campaign in Great Britain. It would take thirty years of tireless efforts in Parliament for abolition to become a reality, but in March 1807 the Bill for the Abolition of Slavery became law. Newton, judging himself too old to actively campaign, contributed to the cause with his first public attack on slavery, a ten-thousand-word essay entitled "Thoughts upon the African Slave Trade." He wrote, "I hope it will always be a subject of humiliating reflection to me, that I was once an active instrument in a business at which my heart now shudders." His wholehearted condemnation of the trade recognized, however, that he was "bound in conscience to take shame to myself by a public confession, which, however sincere, comes too late to prevent or repair the misery and mischief to which I have, formerly, been accessory." Newton had prayed that he would live to see the law passed, which he did. He died in December of 1807.

12

Seafaring Life

In the interval between my first and second voyage after my marriage, I began to keep a sort of diary, a practice that I have since found of great use. I had in this period repeated proofs of the ingratitude and evil of my heart. A life of ease with my friends and the full satisfaction of my desires did not encourage the progress of grace.

Yet, upon the whole, I gained ground. I became acquainted with books that gave me a further view of Christian doctrine and experience, particularly Scougall's *Life of God in the Soul of Man*, Hervey's *Meditations*, and *Life of Colonel Gardiner*. I heard only the common sort of preaching nor did I benefit from a Christian acquaintance. I was likewise greatly hindered by a cowardly, reserved spirit for I was afraid of being thought overly scrupulous. Though I could not live without prayer, I did not propose it even to my wife until she herself urged me to. I had little of the zeal and love that seem so suitable in the case of one who has had much forgiven. When the next season called me abroad again, I sailed from Liverpool on a new ship in July 1752.

A seafaring life of necessity lacks the benefit of public worship and Christian fellowship. In other respects, however, I do not know any calling that affords a greater advantage to an awakened soul for promoting the life of God in the soul, especially for a person who has the command of a ship. He has the power to restrain gross sin in others and to manage his own time. It was more so in African voyages since these ships carry a double number of men and officers compared to most other ships. This made my responsibilities very easy and, except for the occasional bustle of trade on the coast, allowed me leisure time.

Divine Providence and Communion

In these circumstances, one is out of the reach of innumerable temptations and, if so inclined, has opportunity to observe the wonders of God in the great deeps. The two noblest objects of sight, the expanded sky and the expanded ocean, are continually in view. Incidences of divine providence, in answer to prayer, occur almost every day. All these help to renew and confirm the life of faith. For a religious sailor they greatly compensate for the lack of spiritual opportunities that can be enjoyed only upon the shore. Although my knowledge of spiritual things was at this time very small, I sometimes look back with fondness upon these scenes. I never knew sweeter or more frequent hours of divine communion than in my two last voyages to Guinea, when I was almost secluded from company on shipboard or when on shore among the natives.

I have wandered through the woods, reflecting on the singular goodness of the Lord to me, in a place where perhaps there was not a person that knew Him for a thousand miles around me. Often on these occasions, I have restored the beautiful lines of Propertius to their right owner. They are full of blasphemy and madness when addressed to a creature but full of comfort and wholesomeness when spoken by a believer:

In desert wood, with Thee, my God,
Where human footsteps never trod,
How happy could I be!
Thou my repose from care, my Light
Amidst the darkness of the night,
In solitude my company.[1]

Slave Trading

In the course of this voyage I was wonderfully preserved in the midst of many obvious yet unforeseen dangers. At one time there was a conspiracy among my own crew to become pirates and take the ship from me. When the plot was nearly ripe and they waited for a convenient opportunity, two of the plotters were taken ill one day. One of them died, and he was the only person I buried while on board. This suspended the affair and led to its discovery; otherwise the consequences might have been fatal.

The slaves on board were likewise frequently plotting insurrections. Sometimes they were upon the very brink of rioting, but it was always disclosed in due time. When I thought myself most secure, I was suddenly alarmed with danger; and when I almost despaired of life, a sudden deliverance was given to me.

Frequently Near Death

At one time I was at a place called Mana, near Cape Mount, where I had conducted sizeable business transactions. I had some debts and accounts to settle, which required my presence on shore, and I intended to go the next morning. I left the ship, as I had planned, but when I came near the shore, the surf ran so high that I was afraid to attempt a landing. I had often attempted to land at a worse time, but I felt an inward hindrance and unwillingness I could not explain. The surf furnished an excuse, and after hesitating for about half an hour, I returned to the ship without doing my business. This is something I never did except for that morning in all the time I was involved in trade.

I soon learned the reason for all this. The day before I intended to land, a scandalous and groundless accusation was made against me—by whose instigation I could never learn—that greatly threatened my honor and interest, both in Africa and England. It would perhaps, humanly speaking, have threatened my life, if I had landed according to my plan. I was very uneasy for a few hours but was soon comforted. I heard no more of this accusation until the next voyage when it was publicly acknowledged to be a malicious slander without the least merit.

Such were the vicissitudes and difficulties through which the Lord preserved me. Faith and patience were often exercised but suitable strength was also given. Since such things did not occur every day, the study of the Latin was renewed and carried on from time to time when business would permit. I was usually very regular in the management of my time. I allotted eight hours for sleep and meals, eight hours for exercise and devotion, and eight hours for my books. Thus, by varying my schedule, the whole day was agreeably filled up, and I seldom found a day too long or an hour to spare. My studies kept me occupied; otherwise they were hardly worth the time they cost since they led me to an admiration of false models and false maxims, an almost unavoidable consequence of admiring classic authors.

From the coast I went to St. Christopher's. Here my idolatrous heart was its own punishment. The letters I expected from Mrs. Newton were by mistake forwarded to Antigua, which had been at first proposed as our port. Since I was certain of her punctuality in writing, if alive, I concluded that, by not hearing from her, she was surely dead. This fear affected me more and more. I lost my appetite and felt an incessant pain in my stomach. In about three weeks' time I was under the weight of an imaginary blow.

I felt the severe symptoms of that mixture of pride and madness that is commonly called a broken heart. Indeed I wonder that it is not more common than it appears to be. How often do the potsherds of the earth presume to contend with their Maker! What a wonder of mercy it is that they are not all broken! However, my lament was not all grief; conscience had a share. I thought my unfaithfulness to God had deprived me of her, especially my backwardness in speaking of spiritual things, which I could hardly attempt even to her.

The thought that I had lost invaluable, irrecoverable opportunities, which both duty and love should have motivated me to make use of, stung me. I thought I would have given the world to know that she was living so that I might at least fulfill my obligations by writing, even though I was never to see her again. This was a hard lesson, but I hope it did some good. After I had suffered for some weeks, I thought of sending a small vessel to Antigua. I did so, and it brought me several packets. These restored my health and peace and showed me the strong contrast between the Lord's goodness to me and my unbelief and ingratitude toward Him.

In August 1753, I returned to Liverpool. My stay at home after that voyage was very short—only six weeks. In that time nothing very memorable occurred. I will therefore continue with an account of my third and last voyage.

Endnote

1. The Latin poet Propertius, (50?–?15 B.C.) was known mainly for his romantic poetry, of which some 4000 lines in four books have survived. His first book of poems (c. 25 B.C.) was dedicated to his mistress. Newton paraphrases the pagan poet's thoughts to focus the sentiments upon God, who is the true source of the inspiration that Newton found in solitude and nature.

13

Leaving the Seafaring Life

Before I sailed on my third voyage, I met a young man who had formerly been a midshipman and my close companion on board the *Harwich*. He was, at the time I first knew him, a temperate youth. I found my unhappy attempts to infect him with libertine principles had been too successful. When we met at Liverpool, our acquaintance was renewed with the same level of intimacy. He had a good mind and had read many good books. Our conversation frequently turned to religion, and I very much wanted to repair the damage I had done to him. I gave him a clear account of the manner and reason for my change and used every argument to persuade him to relinquish his infidel beliefs. When I sometimes pressed him to the point of having no answer, he would remind me that I was the first person who had given him an idea of freedom. This was the cause of many sad reflections on my part.

He was then going as a master to Guinea; but before his ship was ready, his merchant went bankrupt, which canceled the voyage. Since he didn't expect to find another position that year, I offered to take him with me as a companion so that he might learn more about the coast. The gentleman who employed me promised to provide a position for him upon his return. My motivation was not so much as to help him in his business but to have an opportunity of discussing religion with him at leisure. I hoped that in the course of the voyage, my arguments, example, and prayers might have some good effect on him.

My intention in this decision was better than my judgment, and I had many reasons later to regret it. He was terribly profane and grew worse and worse. I saw in him a living picture of what I had once been. It was very uncomfortable to have it always before my eyes.

He was not only deaf to my protest himself, but also worked as hard as he could to counteract my influence upon others. He was impulsive and easily angered, and it required all my care and authority to hold him in any degree of control. He was a sharp thorn in my side for some time. Finally I had an opportunity on the coast to buy a small vessel which I supplied with a cargo from my own ship. I gave him the command and sent him away to trade on behalf of the ship.

When we parted I forcefully repeated my best advice to him. I believe his friendship and regard for me were as great as could be expected since our beliefs were so diametrically opposed. He seemed greatly affected when I left him, but my words had no weight. When he found himself free from my supervision, he indulged every appetite. His violent intemperance, added to the heat of the climate, threw him into a malignant fever, which killed him in a few days. He died convinced, but not changed.

The account I had from those who were with him was dreadful. His rage and despair struck them all with horror. He pronounced his own fatal doom before he expired, without any appearance that he either hoped or asked for mercy. I thought it not improper to give you this stark contrast, as a stronger illustration of the goodness of God to me, the chief of sinners.

I left the coast in about four months and sailed for St. Christopher's. Until now I had enjoyed a perfect state of health in different climates for several years. On this passage, however, I came down with a fever that put me at death's door. My letters from this period, when I could hardly hold a pen, show that I thought that I would never write again. I did not have the "full assurance" that is so desirable at a time when flesh and heart fail. But my hopes were greater than my fears, and I felt a silent composure of spirit that enabled me to endure the event without much anxiety.

"Able to Save to the Uttermost"

My trust, though weak in degree, was fixed upon the blood and righteousness of Jesus. The words, "He is able to save to the uttermost" (Heb. 7:25), gave me great relief. I was for a while troubled with a particular thought. I do not know whether it was a temptation or whether the fever had disordered my mind. I seemed not so much afraid of God's anger and punishment as I was of being lost and overlooked amid the myriads continually entering the unseen world. What is my soul, thought I, among such an innumerable multitude? Perhaps the Lord will not take notice of me. I was perplexed thus for some time; but at last a text of Scripture occurred to my mind and put an end to the doubt: "The Lord knoweth them that are His" (2 Tim. 2:19). In about ten days, when those about me had lost hope, I began to mend. By the time of our arrival in the West Indies, I was perfectly recovered.

A Christian Captain

For about six years, the Lord was pleased to lead me in a secret way. I had learned something of the evil of my heart. I had read the Bible over and over along with several good books. I had a general view of gospel truths. My concepts were in many respects, however, confused. In all this time I did not meet with one acquaintance who could answer my questions.

Upon my arrival at St. Christopher's, I found a ship's captain from London whose conversation was very helpful to me. He was a man of experience in the things of God and of a lively disposition. We discovered each other by some casual conversation in mixed company, and soon became, so far as business would permit, inseparable. For nearly a month we spent every evening together on board each other's ship alternately and often prolonged our visits until almost daybreak. I was all ear; he not only increased my understanding, but his teaching warmed my heart. He encouraged me to pray aloud in gatherings, and he taught me the benefit of Christian conversation. He helped me resolve to make my profession more public and to attempt to speak for God.

From him, rather from the Lord by him, I received an increase in knowledge. My beliefs became clearer and more evangelical. I was delivered from a fear that had long troubled me—the fear of relapsing into my former sin. Now I began to understand the security of the covenant of grace and to expect to be preserved, not by my own power and holiness but by the mighty power and promise of God through faith in an unchangeable Savior.

My friend likewise gave me a general view of the heresies and controversies of the times, of which I had no knowledge, and finally directed me where to inquire in London for further instruction. With these newly-acquired advantages, I left him, and my passage home gave me leisure to digest what I had received. I had much comfort and freedom during those seven weeks, and my sun was seldom clouded. I arrived in Liverpool during August 1754.

His View of the Slave Trade

By the beginning of November I was again ready to put to sea, but the Lord saw fit to overrule my plans. During the time I was engaged in the slave trade, I never had the least scruple as to its lawfulness. I was more or less satisfied with it as the appointment that God's providence had marked out for me. It was a usually very profitable business, although not in my case. The Lord knew that a great wealth would not be good for me.

I considered myself as a sort of jailer, and I was sometimes shocked with an occupation that was perpetually connected with chains, bolts, and shackles. Because of this I had often prayed that the Lord in His own time would be pleased to place me in a more humane calling where I might have more frequent fellowship with His people and worship. I longed to be freed from these long separations from home, which were very often hard to bear. My prayers were answered, though in a way I had never expected.

I was within two days of sailing and, to all appearances, in good health as usual. In the afternoon I was sitting with Mrs. Newton, drinking tea and talking over past events, when I was overcome with a seizure. I was left unconscious and motionless, with no sign of life but that of breathing. It lasted about an hour.

When I recovered, a pain and dizziness in my head convinced the physicians to judge it would not be safe or prudent for me to proceed on the voyage. On the advice of my friend to whom the ship belonged, I resigned my command the day before she sailed. Thus I was unexpectedly called from that service and freed from the consequences of that voyage. The person who went in my place, most of the officers, and many of the crew died, and the vessel was brought home with great difficulty.[1]

Mrs. Newton's Illness

Now disengaged from business, I left Liverpool and spent most of the following year at London and in Kent. I then experienced a new trial. You can easily understand that Mrs. Newton was not an unconcerned spectator when I was taken ill. The blow that struck me reached her in the same instant, but she did not feel it until her apprehensions on my account began to subside. As I grew better, she was thrown into a disorder that no physician could define or medicines remove. Without any of the ordinary symptoms of consumption, she decayed almost visibly.[2] She became so weak that she could hardly bear anyone to walk across the room she was in. I was placed for about eleven months in what Dr. Young calls the "dreadful post of observation, darker every hour."

After my settlement at Liverpool, the Lord was pleased to restore Mrs. Newton by His own hand, when all hopes from medical treatment seemed futile. Before this took place, however, I have some other incidents to mention.

Endnotes

1. A Captain Potter, who replaced Newton on the voyage, was killed along with two others when slaves took over the ship off the African coast.
2. "Consumption" was the common term for tuberculosis, which would have been accompanied by other symptoms as well.

14

A Student of Scripture

Following the directions I had received from my friend at St. Kitts, I soon found religious acquaintances in London. I usually attended Mr. Brewer's ministry when in town. From him I received much help, both in public and private, for he was pleased to favor me with his friendship. His kindness and the close friendship between us continued and increased. Of all my many friends I am most deeply indebted to him.

The late Mr. H— was my second acquaintance, a man of choice spirit and abundant zeal for the Lord's service. I enjoyed his correspondence until near the time of his death. Upon Mr. Whitefield's return from America, my two good friends introduced me to him. Although I had little personal acquaintance with him until afterward, his ministry was exceedingly helpful to me. I had likewise access to some religious societies and came to know many excellent Christians in private life.

When at London, therefore, I lived at the fountainhead of spiritual benefits. When I was in Kent, it was very different. Though I found some serious persons there, the fine, varied woodland country afforded me advantages of another kind. I passed at least a few hours every day in solitude when the weather was fair—

sometimes in the thickest woods and sometimes on the highest hills where almost every step brought a change in scenery. It has been my habit for many years to perform my devotional exercises outdoors when I have opportunity. These rural scenes tend to both refresh and calm my spirits. A beautiful, diversified landscape gladdens my heart. When I am away from the noise and insignificant works of men, I consider myself to be in the great temple that the Lord has built for His own honor.

The Lord's Comfortable Presence

The country between Rochdale and Maidstone, bordering upon the Medway, was well suited to my frame of mind. Were I to go over it now, I could point to many different places where I have either earnestly sought or happily found the Lord's comfortable presence with my soul. I lived sometimes at London and sometimes in the country until the autumn of the following year. All this while I had two trials more or less upon my mind. The first and principal was Mrs. Newton's illness. She grew worse, and each day I had more reason to fear that the hour of separation was at hand. Exercising my faith, I was in some measure resigned to the Lord's will; but too often my heart rebelled, and I found it hard either to trust or to submit.

I likewise had some concern about my future. The African trade was overworked that year, and my friends did not care to fit out another ship until mine returned. I had some apprehension, but having food and clothing has seldom been a cause of great concern to me. I found it easier to trust the Lord for them than for a position, but this prayer was answered first.

Tide Surveyor at Liverpool

In August I received word that I had been nominated for the office of tide surveyor.[1] Such positions are usually obtained, or at least sought, with much effort, but this came to me unsought and unexpected. I knew that my good friends in Liverpool had endeavored to procure another post for me but found it taken. I found out afterwards that the place I had missed would have been very unsuitable for me. This, which I had no thought of, was the very thing I would have wished for. It gave me plenty of leisure and the freedom to live in my own way. The good hand of the Lord was in this event.

While excited by this future prospect, my distress in my present circumstances was doubled. I was obliged to leave Mrs. Newton in the greatest extremity of pain and illness. The physicians could do no more, and I had no reason to believe that I would see her again alive—but nothing is impossible with the Lord. I had a severe conflict, but faith prevailed. I found the promise of strength proportioned to my need remarkably fulfilled. The day before I set out, and not until then, the burden was entirely taken from my mind. I was strengthened to commit both her and myself to the Lord's disposal and departed from her in a cheerful frame. Soon after I was gone, she began to mend. She recovered so fast, that in about two months I had the pleasure to meet her at Stone on her journey to Liverpool.

Since October 1755, we have been comfortably settled at Liverpool, and all my circumstances have been remarkably free of worry. My trials have been light and few, but I still find that a life of faith is a daily necessity.

His Principal Trial

My principal trial is the body of sin and death, which makes me often sigh out the apostle's complaint, "O wretched man that I am!" (Rom. 7:24). With him likewise I can say, "I thank God through Jesus Christ our Lord" (v. 25). I live in a barren land, where the knowledge of and power of the gospel is very low, yet here are a few of the Lord's people. This has been a useful school for me, where I have studied more deliberately the truths I gathered up in London.

I brought with me a considerable supply of intellectual truth, but I have found that there is no effectual teacher but God. We can receive no more than He is pleased to communicate. No knowledge is truly useful except that which is made by experience. Many things I thought I had learned would not stand up in the face of temptation until I had in this way learned them over again. Since the year 1757, I have had an increasing number of friends in the West Riding of Yorkshire, where the gospel has grown considerably. This has been a good school for me; I have conversed at large among all groups without joining any. In my attempts to hit the golden mean, I have sometimes been drawn too near the different extremes; yet the Lord has enabled me to profit by my mistakes. I am still a learner, and the Lord still condescends to teach me. I have accomplished only a very little; but I trust in Him to carry on His work in my soul and by His grace and providence to increase my knowledge of Him and of myself.

Divorced from the Classics

When I was settled in a house and found my business would give me considerable free time, I considered how I might make the most of it. Determined "to know nothing but Jesus Christ and Him crucified" (1 Cor. 2:2), I resolved to pursue nothing that did not serve this main purpose. This resolution divorced me, as I have already hinted, from the classics and mathematics. My first attempt was to learn enough Greek to enable me to understand the New Testament and Septuagint. When I had made some progress in this study, I began studying Hebrew the following year. Two years afterwards, having seen some advantage in reading from the Syriac version, I began studying that language.

I have not attained or ever aimed at a critical skill in any of these languages. I had no goal for them except in reference to something else. I only wanted the meaning of scriptural words and phrases, and for this I availed myself of others who had endured the drudgery before me. I can read in Hebrew the historical books and Psalms somewhat proficiently. In the Prophets, I am frequently obliged to consult the lexicons. However, I am able, with such helps as are at hand, to judge for myself the meaning of any passage I may consult. Beyond this there are better uses of my time. I would rather be useful to others than die with the reputation of an eminent linguist.

Together with these studies I have kept up a course of reading of the best writers in theology that I can find, in Latin and English, and some French, which I picked up at times while I was at sea. But in these two or three years I have given myself chiefly to writing and have not found time to read many books besides the Scriptures.

In all my literary attempts, I have been obliged to strike out on my own path by the light I acquired from books since I have not had a teacher or assistant since I was ten years old.

His Desire to Serve the Lord

I have told you that it was my dear mother's hope that I would enter the ministry. Her death, and the life in which I afterward engaged, seemed to cut off that probability. The first desires of this sort in my own mind arose from my reflection on Galatians 1:23–24: "But they had heard only, that he which persecuted us in times past now preached the faith which once he destroyed. And they glorified God in me." I wished for such a public opportunity to testify to the riches of divine grace. I thought I was, more than most others, a fit person to proclaim the faithful saying that "Jesus Christ came into the world to save the chief of sinners" (1 Tim. 1:15). Since my life had been full of remarkable turns and I seemed selected to show what the Lord could do, I had some hope that perhaps sooner or later He might call me into His service.

It was this hope that made me determined to study the original Scriptures, but it remained an imperfect desire until it was recommended to me by some Christian friends. I questioned the thought when it was first seriously proposed to me, but afterward I set apart some weeks to consider the case, consult my friends, and pray for the Lord's direction. The judgment of my friends and many things that occurred tended to convince me.

My first thought was to join the Dissenters, but I preferred the Established Church in some respects.[2] I asked to be ordained by the late Archbishop of York. As you may guess, I met with a refusal. At present (1763) my desire to serve the Lord is not weakened, but I am not as hasty to push myself forward as I was formerly. It is sufficient that He knows how to make use of me and that He both can and will do what is best. To Him I commend myself. I trust that His will and my true interest are inseparable. To His name be glory.

Endnotes

1. A position in the Customs Office. Newton was responsible for a sizeable office and for the inspection of arriving ships to insure import duties were paid.
2. The state church or Church of England.

The parish church of St. Peter and St. Paul, Olney, where John Newton first began his ministry (photo courtesy of the Cowper and Newton Museum, Olney).

Appendix 1

A FURTHER ACCOUNT OF NEWTON'S LIFE

Near the end of his narrative, Newton relates that which motivated him to seek a regular appointment to the ministry in the Church of England and mentions the refusal he met with in his first attempt.[1] On December 16, 1758, Mr. Newton applied to the Archbishop of York for ordination. The Bishop of Chester, having countersigned his testimonials, directed him to Dr. Newton, the archbishop's chaplain. He was then referred to the secretary, who informed him that he had "represented the matter to the archbishop, but his Grace was inflexible in supporting the rules and canons of the Church."

Newton had done some preaching or expounding at Liverpool, and many encouraged him to take on a more widespread itinerant ministry. He was so inclined, and he expresses his motives in a letter to his wife.

> The death of the late Rev. Mr. Jones of St. Savior's has pressed this concern more closely upon my mind. I fear it must be wrong, after having so solemnly devoted myself to the Lord

Newton was ordained and served the parish of Olney.

for His service, to wear away my time, and bury my talents in silence, because I have been refused orders in the Established Church after all the great things He has done for me. … The exercises of my mind upon this point, I believe, have not been peculiar to myself. I have known several persons, sensible, pious, of competent abilities, and cordially attached to the Established Church, who, being wearied out with repeated refusals of ordination, and perhaps, not having the advantage of such an adviser as I had, have at length struck into the itinerant path, or settled among the Dissenters. Some of these, yet living, are men of respectable characters, and useful in their ministry.

Appointed to the Parish of Olney

In the year 1764, Newton had the curacy[2] of Olney proposed to him and was recommended by Lord Dartmouth to Dr. Green, Bishop of Lincoln, who ordained him.[3] In the parish of Olney he found many who had evangelical views of the truth and had long walked in the light and experience of it. The vicarage was in the gift of the earl of Dartmouth, the nobleman to whom he addressed the first twenty-six letters in his *Cardiphonia*. The earl was a man of sincere devotion and most amiable disposition; he had previously appointed the Rev. Moses Brown as vicar of Olney. Mr. Brown was an evangelical minister and a good man. He had given wholesome instruction to the parishioners of Olney and had been instrumental in the sound conversion in many of them. Newton continued at Olney for nearly sixteen years prior to his transfer to St. Mary Woolnoth in London, to which he was presented by John Thornton.

Providence seems to have directed Newton to Olney, among other reasons, for the relief of the depressed mind of the poet Cowper.[4] Of great importance also was Newton's close proximity to the Rev. Thomas Scott, then curate of Ravenstone and Weston Underwood, a man whose ministry and writings have since been so useful to mankind.

The Patience of a Christian Under Pain

In 1776, Newton was afflicted with a tumor that had formed on his thigh. As it grew larger and more troublesome, he resolved to undergo the experiment of surgical removal. This obliged him to go to London for the operation, which was successfully performed. The painful operation itself was not a trial to Newton so much as a critical opportunity in which he might fail in demonstrating the patience of a Christian under pain. "I felt," said he, "that being enabled to bear a very painful operation, with tolerable calmness and confidence, was a greater favor granted to me than the deliverance from my malady."

While he was faithfully discharging his duties of watching for the temporal and eternal welfare of his flock, a destructive fire broke out in Olney during October 1777. Mr. Newton took an active part in comforting and relieving the sufferers. He collected money for them.

A minister like Newton, who is aware of the interest of his own soul and that of the souls committed to his charge (as the apostle expresses it, "to save himself, and those that hear him), he will undoubtedly experience the reality of Paul's declaration, "Yea, all that will live godly in Christ Jesus shall suffer persecution" (2 Tim. 3:12), in one form of it or another.

I have heard him say on such an occasion, "When God is about to perform any great work, He generally permits some great opposition to it. Suppose Pharaoh had acquiesced in the departure of the children of Israel, or that they had met with no difficulties in the way. They would, indeed, have passed from Egypt into Canaan with ease, but they, as well as the Church in all future ages, would have been great losers. The wonder-working God would not have been in those extremities, which make His arm so visible. A smooth passage here would have made but a poor story."

But under such difficulties, he never was tempted, to my knowledge, to depart from the precept and example of his Master. He continued to bless them that persecuted him, knowing that "the servant of the Lord must not strive, but be gentle unto all men, apt to teach, patient" (2 Tim. 2:24). To the last day he spent among them, he went straight forward, "in meekness instructing those that opposed, if God peradventure might give them repentance to the acknowledging of the truth" (v. 25).

His Literary Work

Before we take leave of Olney, the reader must be informed of another part of his labors. He had published a volume of sermons in Liverpool dated January 1, 1760. In 1762 he published his *Omicron,* to which his letters, signed Vigil, were afterward annexed. In 1764 appeared his *Narrative.* In 1767 a volume of sermons, preached at Olney. In 1769 his *Review of Ecclesiastical History;* and in 1770 a volume of hymns, of which some were composed by Mr. Cowper and identified by a "C" prefixed to them. To these succeeded, in 1781, his valuable work *Cardiphonia.*

At St. Mary Woolnoth

From Olney, Newton moved to the united parishes of St. Mary Woolnoth and St. Mary Woolchurch Haw, Lombard Street, on the presentation of his friend, Mr. Thornton.

Some difficulty arose concerning Mr. Thornton's right of presentation, the latter being claimed by a nobleman. The question was, therefore, at length brought before the House of Lords and determined in favor of Mr. Thornton.[5] Newton preached his first sermon in these parishes, December 19, 1779, from Ephesians 4:15, "speaking the truth in love." It contained an affectionate address to his parishioners and was immediately published for their use.

Placed in the center of London in an opulent neighborhood, he had now a course of service to pursue that was quite different from his former at Olney. Being well acquainted with the Word of God and the heart of man, he proposed no new weapons of warfare for pulling down the strongholds of sin and Satan around him.

The Importance of His New Sphere

I have heard him speak with great feeling of this last important ministry.

That one of the most ignorant, the most miserable, and the most abandoned of slaves should be plucked from his forlorn state of exile on the coast of Africa and at length be appointed minister of the parish of the first magistrate of the first city in the world; that he should there not only testify of such grace, but stand up as a singular example and monument of it; that he should be enabled to record it in his history, preaching, and writings to the world at large, is a fact I can contemplate with admiration, but never sufficiently grasp.

This reflection, indeed, was so present in his thinking that he seldom passed a single day anywhere without referring to the strange event in one way or other.

Having a friendly and hospitable disposition, his house was open to Christians of all ranks and denominations. Here, like a father among his children, he used to entertain, encourage, and instruct his friends, especially younger ministers or candidates for the ministry. Here also the poor, the afflicted, and the tempted found an asylum and a sympathy that they could scarcely find to an equal degree anywhere else.

His Timely Hints and Sayings

His timely hints were often given with much effect and profit to the numerous acquaintances who surrounded him in his public position. Some time after he had published his *Omicron* and described the three stages of growth in religion, from the blade, the ear, and the full corn in the ear, distinguishing them by the letters A, B, and C, a conceited young minister wrote to him, telling him that he read his own character accurately drawn in that of C. Newton wrote in reply, that in drawing the character of C, or full maturity, he had forgotten to add, until now, one prominent feature of C's character, namely, that C never knew his own face.

"It grieves me," said he, on another occasion, "to see so few of my wealthy parishioners come to church. I always consider the rich as under greater obligation to the preaching of the gospel than the poor. For at church, the rich must hear the whole truth as well as others. There they have no escape. But let them once get home, you will be troubled to get at them. When you are admitted, you are so fettered with formality, so interrupted and damped with the frivolous conversation of their friends, that, as Archbishop Leighton says, 'it is well if your visit does not prove a blank or a blot.'"

He would make use of every occurrence that he could, with propriety, bring into the pulpit. One night he found a notice put up at St. Mary Woolnoth's upon which he commented a great deal when he came to preach. The notice was to this effect: "A young man, having come into the possession of a very considerable fortune, desires the prayers of the congregation, that he may be preserved from the snares to which it exposes him." "Now if the man," said Newton, "had lost a fortune, the world would not have wondered to have seen him put up a notice; but this man has been better taught."

Coming out of his church on a Wednesday, a lady stopped him on the steps and said, "The ticket, of which I held a quarter, has drawn a prize of ten thousand pounds. I know you will congratulate me upon this occasion." "Madam," said he, "as for a friend under temptation, I will endeavor to pray for you."

I could not help observing one day how much he was grieved with the mistake of a minister who appeared to pay too much attention to politics. "For my part," he said, "I have no temptation to turn politician, and much less to inflame a party in these times. When a ship is leaky and a mutinous spirit divides the company on board, a wise man would say, 'My good friends, while we are debating, the water is gaining on us; we had better leave the debate and go to the pumps.' I endeavor," he continued, "to turn my people's eyes from instruments to God. I am continually attempting to show them how far they are from knowing either the matter of fact or the matter of right. I teach our great privileges in this country and advise a discontented man to take a lodging for a little while in Russia or Prussia."

I remember to have heard him say, when speaking of his continual interruptions, "I see in this world two heaps of human happiness and misery; now if I can take but the smallest bit from one heap and add to the other, I carry a point. If, as I go home, a child has dropped a penny and if, by giving it another, I can wipe away tears, I feel I have done something. I would be glad indeed to do greater things, but I will not neglect this. When I hear a knock at my study door, I hear a message from God. It may be a lesson of instruction, perhaps a lesson of patience; but since it is His message, it must be interesting."

But it was not merely under his own roof that his benevolent aims were so exerted. He was always ready to take an active part in relieving the destitute, counseling the distressed, or restoring the prodigal, in whatever state or place he discovered one.

The Hand of God in Every Event

Newton used to spend a month or two annually at the house of a friend in the country. He always took an affectionate leave of his congregation before he departed and spoke of his return as uncertain, considering the variety of incidents which might prevent it. Nothing was more remarkable than his constant habit of regarding the hand of God in every event, however trivial it might appear to others. On every occasion, in the concerns of every hour, in matters public or private, like Enoch, he "walked with God" (Gen. 5:22).

Newton experienced a severe shock soon after he came to St. Mary's in the death of his niece, Miss Eliza Cunningham. He loved her with the affection of a parent, and she was, indeed, truly lovely. With the most amiable natural qualities, she possessed a sincere spiritual devotion. Mr. and Mrs. Newton saw her gradually sink into death. Fully prepared to meet her heavenly Father, she departed October 6, 1785, aged fourteen years and eight months.

But "clouds return after the rain"—a greater loss than that of Miss Cunningham was to follow. These memoirs show the more than ordinary affection Newton felt for her who had been so long his idol, as he used to call her. I shall add but one more instance, out of many that might easily be collected.

Being with him at the house of a lady at Blackheath, we stood at a window which had a view of Shooter's Hill. "Ah," he said, "I remember the many journeys I took from London to stand at the top of that hill, in order to look toward the part in which Mrs. Newton then lived. I could not see the spot itself after traveling several miles, for she lived far beyond what I could see from the hill. But it gratified me even to look toward the spot, and this I did always once and sometimes twice a week."

"Why," I said, "this is more like one of the vagaries of romance than of real life."

"True," he replied, "but real life has extravagances that would not be permitted to appear in a well written romance."

With such a constant attachment, it is evident how keenly he must have felt it as he observed the progress of her illness. This will be manifest from the following account that was added to his publication, *Letters to a Wife:*

Some Facts Regarding the Cause, Progress, and Close of the Last Illness of My Late Dear Wife

My dear wife had naturally a good constitution and was favored with good spirits to the last. But she sustained a violent shock in the year 1754 when I was suddenly attacked by a seizure (I know not of what kind) which left me for about an hour with no sign of life but breathing. This made a sudden change in her and subjected her from that time to a variety of chronic ailments. I believe she spent ten years out of the forty that she was spared to me (if all the days of her sufferings were added together) in illness. But she had likewise long intervals of health.

Before our move from Liverpool, she received a blow upon her left breast. This occasioned her some pain and anxiety for a little time, but it soon wore off. A small lump remained, but I heard no more of it for many years. Her tenderness for me made her conceal it as long as possible. I have often since wondered at her success, and how I could be kept so long ignorant.

In October 1788, she applied, unknown to me, to a friend of mine, an eminent surgeon. Her plan was, if he approved it, to submit to an operation. She planned to so arrange with him that it might be performed in my absence and before I could know of it. But the surgeon told her that the malady was too far advanced. The tumor, the size of half a melon, was too large to be removed without danger of her life. The only advice he could give her was to keep herself as quiet and her mind as easy as possible. The pains to which she was exposed were generally rendered tolerable by the use of laudanum; to which, however, she had a dislike, little short of an hatred.

I cannot easily describe the composure and resignation with which she gave me this account the day after her interview with the surgeon nor the sensations of my mind while I heard it. My conscience told me that I well deserved to be wounded where I was most sensitive and that it was my duty to submit with silence to the will of the Lord. But I strongly felt that, unless He was pleased to give me this submission, I was more likely to toss like a wild bull in a net, in defiance of my better judgment.

Soon after, the Lord was pleased to visit our dear adopted daughter with a dreadful fever. She (Miss Catlett) was brought very near to the grave indeed. We once or twice thought her dead. But He, who in judgment remembers mercy, restored her and still preserves her, to be the chief earthly comfort of my old age.

This heavy trial lasted throughout a very severe winter. This by no means promoted the tranquility of mind that my good friend wished my dear wife to preserve. She was often greatly fatigued and distraught. Next to each other, this dear child had the nearest place both in her heart and mine. The effects were soon apparent. As the spring of 1789 advanced, her illness rapidly increased. Her pains were almost incessant and often intense, and she could seldom lie one hour in bed in the same position. Oh! my heart, what didst thou suffer!

But in April God mercifully afforded relief, and gave such a blessing to the means employed that her pains ceased. Though I believe she never had an hour of perfect ease, she felt little of the distressing pains incident to her illness from that time to the end of her life.

In the close of the summer she was able to go to Southampton. She returned tolerably well, and was twice at church the first week after she came home. She then went no more out, except in a coach for a little air and exercise; but she was cheerful, tolerably easy, slept as well as most people who are in perfect health, and could receive and converse with her kind friends who visited her.

Under this trying discipline I learned more than ever to pity those whose sufferings are aggravated by poverty. Our distress was not small, yet we had everything within reach that could in any degree refresh or relieve. We had faithful and affectionate servants who were always willingly engaged, even beyond their power, in attending and assisting her by night and by day. What must be the feelings of those who, when afflicted with grievous diseases, pine away, unpitied, unnoticed, without help, and in a great measure destitute of common necessaries? This reflection, among others, helped to quiet my mind, and to convince me that I had much more cause for thankfulness than for complaint.

For about a year her spirits were good, her patience was exemplary. There was a cheerfulness in her looks and her language that was wonderful. Often the liveliness of her remarks has forced a smile upon us, when the tears were in our eyes. Whatever little contrivances she formed for her amusement in the course of the day, she would attend to nothing until she had finished her stated reading of the Scripture, to which she gave much time and attention.

I have her Bible in which almost every principal text, from the beginning to the end, is marked in the margin with a pencil, by her own dear hand. The good Word of God was her medicine and her food while she was able to read it. She read Dr. Watts's Psalms and Hymns, and the Olney Hymns, in the same manner.

There are few of them in which one, two, or more verses are not thus marked. In many, which I suppose she read more frequently, every verse is marked.

One addition to our trial remained. It had been her custom, when she went from her sofa to her bed, to exert herself for my encouragement, to show me how well she could walk. But it pleased the Lord that, by some alteration that affected her spine, she was unable to move herself. Other circumstances rendered it extremely difficult to move her. It has taken five of us nearly two hours to move her from one side of the bed to the other. At times, even this was impracticable, so that she had lain more than a week exactly in the same spot.

All this was necessary on my account. The rod had a voice, and it was the voice of the Lord. I understood the meaning no less plainly than if He had spoken audibly from heaven, and said, "Now contemplate your idol! Now see what *she* is, whom you once presumed to prefer to *Me!*"

Even this bitter cup was sweetened by the patience and resignation that He gave her. When I would say, "You suffer greatly," her answer usually was, "I suffer indeed; but, not greatly." And she often expressed her thankfulness that, though her body was immovable, she was still permitted the use of her hands.

One of the last concerns she felt in this world was when my honored friend, patron, and benefactor, the late John Thornton, Esq. was removed to a better one. She revered him, I believe, more than she did any person upon earth, and she had reason. Few had nearer access to know and admire his character, and perhaps none were under greater, if equal, obligations to him than we. She knew of his illness but was always afraid to inquire after the event nor should I have ventured to inform her. But the occasion requiring me to leave her for four or five hours, when I hardly expected to find her alive at my return, I was constrained to give her the reason of my absence.

She eagerly replied, "Go, by all means; I would not have you stay with me upon any consideration." I put the funeral ring I was favored with into her hands; she put it first to her lips, and then to her eyes, bedewing it with her tears. She survived him just more than a month.

Her mind became so affected that I could do little more than sit and look at her. Our communication by words was nearly broken off. She could not easily bear the sound of the gentlest foot upon the carpet nor of the softest voice. On Sunday, December 12, when I was preparing for church in the morning, she sent for me, and we took a final farewell. She faintly uttered an endearing name, which was familiar to her and gave me her hand, which I held, while I prayed by her bedside. We exchanged a few tears, but I was almost as unable to speak as she was. I returned soon after and said, "If your mind, as I trust, is in a state of peace, it will be a comfort to me if you can signify it by holding up your hand." She held it up and waved it to and fro several times.

That evening, her speech, her sight, and, I believe, her hearing wholly failed. She continued perfectly composed, without taking notice of anything or showing any sign of pain or uneasiness until Wednesday evening, toward seven o'clock. She then began to breathe very hard. Her breathing might be called groaning for it was heard in every part of the house; but she lay quite still, with a placid countenance as if in a gentle slumber. There was no start or struggle nor a feature ruffled. I took my post by her bedside and watched her nearly three hours with a candle in my hand until I saw her breathe her last on December 15, 1790, a little before ten in the evening.

When I was sure she was gone, I took off her ring, according to her repeated injunction and put it upon my own finger. I then kneeled down with the servants who were in the room and gave to the Lord my unfeigned thanks for her deliverance and her peaceful passing.

About two or three months before her death, when I was walking up and down the room offering disjointed prayers from a heart torn with distress, a thought suddenly struck me with unusual force. The promises of God must be true. Surely the Lord will help me if I am willing to be helped.

It occurred to me that we are often led, from a vain complacency in what we call our sensibility, to indulge that unprofitable grief, which both our duty and our peace require us to resist to the utmost of our power. I instantly said aloud, "Lord, I am helpless indeed in myself, but I hope I am willing, without reserve, that Thou shouldest help me."

It had been much upon my mind, from the beginning of this trial that I was a minister and that the eyes of many were upon me. In my preaching I had very much endeavored to comfort the afflicted by representing the gospel as an effectual remedy for every evil, a full compensation for every want or loss to those who truly receive it. Though a believer may be afflicted, he cannot be properly unhappy unless he gives way to self-will and unbelief. I had often told my hearers that a trial, if rightly used, was to the Christian a post of honor. It afforded the fairest opportunity of exemplifying the power of divine grace to the praise and glory of the Giver.

It had been my daily prayer that I might not by impatience or despondency, be deprived of confirming, by my own practice, the doctrine that I had preached to others. I prayed that I might not give them occasion to apply to me the words of Eliphaz to Job: "Thy words have upholden him that was falling, and thou hast strengthened the feeble knees. But now it is come upon thee, and thou faintest; it touchest thee, and thou art troubled" (Job 4:4–5).

And I had not prayed in vain. From the time that I so remarkably felt myself willing to be helped, my heart trusted in Him and I was helped indeed. Through the whole of my painful trial, I attended all my stated and occasional services as usual. A stranger would scarcely have discovered either by words or looks, that I was in trouble. Many of our closest friends were apprehensive that this long affliction and especially the final event, would overwhelm me, but it was quite the opposite. It did not prevent me from preaching a single sermon, and I preached on the day of her death.

After she was gone, my willingness to be helped and my desire that the Lord's goodness to me might be observed by others for their encouragement made me unconcerned for some laws of established custom (the breach of which is often more noticed than the violation of God's commands). I was afraid of sitting at home and indulging myself by poring over my loss. Therefore I was seen in the street and visited some of my close friends that very next day. I preached three times while she lay dead.

Some of my brethren kindly offered their assistance, but as the Lord was pleased to give me strength, both of body and mind, I thought it my duty to stand up in my place as before. After she was buried in the vault, I preached her funeral sermon with little more emotion than if it had been for another person. I hope that many of my hearers were comforted in their afflictions by what they saw of the Lord's goodness to me in my time of need. It was well worth standing a while in the fire for such an opportunity of experiencing and exhibiting the power and faithfulness of His promises.

I was not supported by lively sensible consolations, but by being enabled to recall to mind some great and leading truths of the Word of God. I saw what indeed I knew before, but never until then so strongly and clearly perceived, that as a sinner I had no right and as a believer I could have no reason to complain. I considered her as a loan, which He who lent her to me had a right to recall whenever He pleased. As I had deserved to forfeit her every day from the first, it was right for me to be thankful that she was spared so long to me than to give her up with reluctance when called for.

His sovereignty is connected with infinite wisdom and goodness. Consequently, if it were possible for me to alter any part of His plan, I could only spoil it. Such a shortsighted creature as I, so blind to the possible consequences of my own wishes, was not only unworthy but also unable to choose well for himself. It was therefore my great mercy and privilege that the Lord condescended to choose for me. May such considerations powerfully affect the hearts of my readers suffering their own troubles. Then I shall not regret having let the public read that which may seem more proper for the subject of a private letter to a friend.

In the year 1790 Mr. Newton had the honorary degree of D.D. conferred upon him by the University of New Jersey, in America, and the diploma sent to him. He also received a work in two volumes, dedicated to him, with the degree letters added to his name. Mr. Newton wrote the author a grateful acknowledgment for the work, but begged to decline an honor which he never intended to accept. "I am," said he, "as one born out of due time. I have neither the pretension nor wish to honors of this kind. However, therefore, the university may overrate my attainments, and thus show their respect, I must not forget myself; it would be both vain and improper were I to concur in it."

Illness of Miss Elizabeth Catlett

Newton used to make excursions in the summer to different friends in the country, endeavoring to make these visits profitable to them and to their neighbors by his prayers and expositions of the Scriptures at their morning and evening worship. I have heard of some who were first brought to the knowledge of themselves and of God by attending his exhortations on these occasions. Indeed, besides what he undertook in a more stated way at the church, he seldom entered a room but something both profitable and entertaining fell from his lips.

After the death of Miss Cunningham and Mrs. Newton, his companion in these summer excursions was his other niece, Miss Elizabeth Catlett. This young lady who had also been brought up by him and his wife with Miss Cunningham now became the object of his naturally affectionate disposition. She also became quite necessary to him by her services in his latter years. She watched him, walked with him, visited wherever he went. When his sight failed, she read to him, divided his food, and was to him all that a dutiful daughter could be.

But in the year 1801 a nervous disorder seized her, and Newton was obliged to allow her to be separated from him. During the year it lasted, the weight of the affliction, added to his weight of years, seemed to overwhelm him.

Newton's Later Years

It was with a mixture of delight and surprise that friends and hearers of this eminent servant of God beheld him bringing forth fruit in extreme age. Though almost eighty years old, his sight nearly gone and incapable, due to deafness, of joining in conversation; yet his public ministry was regularly continued and maintained with a considerable degree of his former energy. His memory, indeed, was observed to fail but his judgment in divine things still remained. Though some depression of spirit was observed, which he accounted for by his advanced age, his perception, taste, and zeal for the truths he had long received and taught were evident. Like Simeon, having seen the salvation of the Lord, he now only waited and prayed to depart in peace.

After Newton turned eighty, some of his friends feared he might continue his public ministry too long. They noted not only his infirmities in the pulpit, but the decrease of his strength and his occasional depression. On the latter, he observed that he had experienced nothing that in the least affected the principles he had felt and taught. His depressions were the natural result of fourscore years, and that at any age we can only enjoy that comfort from our beliefs which God is pleased to send.

"But," I replied, "in the matter of public preaching, might it not be best to consider your work as done and stop before you evidently discover you can speak no longer?"

"I cannot stop," he said, raising his voice. "What! shall the old African blasphemer stop while he can speak?"[6]

In every future visit I noticed old age making rapid strides. At length his friends found some difficulty in making themselves known to him. His sight, his hearing, and his memory failed. Being mercifully kept from pain, however, he generally appeared easy and cheerful. Whatever he uttered was perfectly consistent with the principles he had so long and so honorably maintained.

Newton declined in this very gradual way until at length it was painful to ask him a question or attempt to rouse faculties almost gone. It is quite natural to ask, although it is not important, how such a decided character left this world. I have heard him say when he has heard particular inquiry made about the last expressions of an eminent believer, "Tell me not how the man died, but how he lived."

Newton's Death

About a month before his death, Mr. Newton said, "It is a great thing to die; and when flesh and heart fail, to have God for the strength of our heart and our portion forever; I know whom I have believed, and He is able to keep that which I have committed unto Him against that day. Henceforth there is laid up for me a crown of righteousness, which the Lord, the righteous Judge, shall give me at that day" (2 Tim. 1:12; 4:8).

Later to his niece, formerly Miss Catlett, he said, "I have been meditating on a subject, 'Come and hear, all ye that fear God, and I will declare what He hath done for my soul'" (Ps. 66:16).

At another time he said, "More light, more love, more liberty. Hereafter I hope, when I shut my eyes on the things of time, I shall open them in a better world. What a thing it is to live under the shadow of the wings of the Almighty! I am going the way of all flesh." And when one replied, "The Lord is gracious," he answered, "If it were not so, how could I dare to stand before Him?"

The following is a copy of the beginning of John Newton's Last Will and Testament, dated June 13, 1803:

"In the name of God, Amen. I, John Newton, of Coleman Street Buildings, in the parish of St. Stephen, Coleman Street, in the city of London, clerk, being through mercy in good health and of sound and disposing mind, memory, and understanding, although in the seventy-eighth year of my age, do for the settling of my temporal concerns, and for the disposal of all the worldly estate which it hath pleased the Lord in His good providence to give me, make this my last will and testament as follows: I commit my soul to my gracious God and Savior, who mercifully spared and preserved me, when I was an apostate, a blasphemer, and an infidel, and delivered me from that state of misery on the coast of Africa into which my obstinate wickedness had plunged me; and Who has been pleased to admit me, though most unworthy, to preach His glorious gospel. I rely with humble confidence upon the atonement, and mediation of the Lord Jesus Christ, God and Man, which I have often proposed to others, as the only foundation whereupon a sinner can build his hope, trusting that He will guard and guide me through the uncertain remainder of my life, and that He will then admit me into His presence in His heavenly kingdom. I would have my body deposited in the vault under the parish church of St. Mary Woolnoth, coffins of my late dear wife and my dear niece, Elizabeth Cunningham; and it is my desire that my funeral may be performed with as little expense as possible, consistent with decency."

The Wednesday before he died, when asked if his mind was at peace, he replied, "I am satisfied with the Lord's will." Newton seemed sensible to his last hour, but expressed nothing remarkable after these words. He died December 21, 1807, and was buried in the vault of his church ten days later, having left the following injunction in a letter for the direction of his executors:

"I propose writing an epitaph for myself, if it may be put up on a plain marble tablet near the vestry door, to the following purport:

JOHN NEWTON, Clerk,
Once an infidel and libertine,
A servant of slaves in Africa,
Was, by the rich mercy of our Lord and Saviour,
JESUS CHRIST,
Preserved, restored, pardoned,
And appointed to preach the faith
He had long laboured to destroy,
Near sixteen years at Olney, in Bucks,
And . . . years in this church.
On February 1, 1750, he married
MARY,
Daughter of the late George Catlett,
of Chatham, Kent,
He resigned her to the Lord who gave her,
On the 15th day of December 1790.

And I earnestly desire that no other monument and no in-scription but to this purport, may be attempted for me."[7]

Endnotes

1. The further details of Newton's life in Appendix 1 and 2 are excerpted from *Memoirs of the Rev. John Newton*, written by his friend and first biographer, Richard Cecil, in 1808.
2. The position of parish clergyman.
3. Lord Dartmouth, a wealthy, politically influential evangelical, as the larg-est landowner in the area of Olney, selected the clergyman for the church. Dartmouth had previously read Newton's expanded letters, given to him by Thomas Haweis. Dartmouth College in New Hampshire would be named after Lord Dartmouth, and it was Dartmouth who gave Newton the use of his large mansion, the Great House in Olney, where "Amazing Grace" was first sung, without instrumental accompaniment. By law only metrical Psalms could be sung in church, so the new hymns of Isaac Watts, Charles Wesley, and John Newton were sung in meeting halls or open air meetings.
4. William Cowper (1731–1800, pronounced "Cooper") suffered from bouts of severe depression and suicidal thoughts throughout much of his life. He collaborated with Newton in the writing of the *Olney Hymns* (published in 1779). Some of his many hymns are "God Moves in a Mys-terious Way" and "O! For a Closer Walk with God." Following the *Olney Hymns*, Cowper found wide acceptance as a poet and became a vigorous opponent of slavery.
5. The dispute was over who had the right to "present" someone to the bishop for the position.
6. Newton's last sermon was preached in October, 1806, for a fund in aid of the widows and orphans of the battle of Trafalgar.
7. Newton's epitaph can still be seen today in the church of St. Mary Woolnoth, but the bodies of John and Mary Newton were reburied in Olney in 1893 due to the construction of the London underground rail system.

Appendix 2

SOME REMARKS BY NEWTON IN FAMILIAR CONVERSATION

When a Christian goes into the world because he sees it is his *call,* yet, while he feels it also his *cross,* it will not hurt him.[1]

Satan will seldom come to a Christian with a gross temptation. A green log and a candle may be safely left together, but bring a few shavings, then some small sticks, and then larger, and you may soon bring the green log to ashes.

If two angels were sent from heaven to execute a divine command, one to conduct an empire and the other to sweep a street in it, they would feel no inclination to change employments.

What some call providential openings, are often powerful temptations; the heart, in wandering, cries, Here is a way opened before me: but, perhaps, not to be trodden but rejected.

A Christian should never plead spirituality for being a sloven. If he be but a shoe cleaner, he should be the best in the parish.

My principal method of defeating heresy is by establishing truth. One proposes to fill a bushel with tares. Now, if I can fill it first with wheat, I shall defy his attempts.

Many have puzzled themselves about the origin of evil. I observe there *is* evil, and that there is a way to escape it, and with this I begin and end.

Consecrated things under the law were first sprinkled with blood, and then anointed with oil, and thenceforward were no more common. Thus under the gospel, every Christian has been a common vessel for profane purposes, but when sprinkled and anointed, he becomes separated and consecrated to God.

A spirit of adoption is the spirit of a child. He may disoblige his father, yet he is not afraid of being turned out of doors. The union is not dissolved although the communion is. He is not well with his father, therefore must be unhappy, as their interests are inseparable.

A Christian in the world is like a man who has had a long intimacy with one, whom at length he finds out to have been the murderer of a kind father. The intimacy, after this, will surely be broken.

Candor will always allow much for inexperience. I have been thirty years forming my own views, and in the course of this time some of my hills have been sinking, and some of my valleys have risen; but how unreasonable would it be to expect all this should take place in another person, and that in the course of a year or two!

Candor forbids us to estimate a character from its accidental blots. Yet it is thus that David and others have been treated.

I can conceive a living man without an arm or a leg, but not without a head or a heart; so there are some truths essential to vital religion and that all awakened souls are taught.

A Christian is like a young nobleman who, on going to receive his estate, is at first enchanted with his prospects. This, in a course of time, may wear off, but a sense of the value of the estate grows daily.

When we first enter into the divine life, we propose to grow rich. God's plan is to make us feel poor.

Good men have need to take heed of building upon groundless impressions. Mr. Whitefield had a son, who, as he imagined, was born to be a very extraordinary man; but the son soon died, and the father was cured of his mistake.

I remember, in going to undertake the care of a congregation, I was reading, as I walked in a green lane, "Fear not, Paul, I have much people in this city." But I soon afterwards was disappointed in finding that Paul was not John and that Corinth was not Warwick.

Christ has taken our nature into heaven to represent us and has left us on earth, with His nature, to represent Him.

Worldly men will be true to their principles, and if we were as true to ours, the visits between the two parties would be short and seldom.

A Christian in the world is like a man transacting his affairs in the rain. He will not suddenly leave his client because it rains; but the moment the business is done, he is off: as it is said in the Acts, "Being let go, they went to their own company."

God deals with us as we do with our children: He first speaks, then gives a gentle stroke, at last a blow.

The religion of a sinner stands on two pillars: namely, what Christ did for us in His flesh and what He performs in us by His Spirit. Most errors arise from an attempt to separate these two.

Man is not taught anything to purpose until God becomes his teacher, and then the glare of the world is put out and the value of the soul rises in full view. A man's present sentiments may not be accurate, but we make too much of sentiments. We pass a field with a few blades. We call it a field of wheat, but here is no wheat. No, not in perfection, but the wheat is sown, and full ears may be expected.

The word "temperance" in the New Testament signifies self-possession. It is a disposition suitable to one who has a race to run and therefore will not load his pockets with lead.

Contrivers of systems on the earth are like contrivers of systems in the heavens: where the sun and moon keep the same course, in spite of the philosophers.

A man always in society is one always on the spend. On the other hand, a mere solitary is, at his best, but a candle in an empty room.

If we were upon the watch for improvement, the common news of the day would furnish it. The falling of the tower of Siloam and the slaughter of the Galileans were the news of the day, which our Lord made use of.

Take away a toy from a child and give him another, and he is satisfied; but if he be hungry, no toy will do. Thus as newborn babes, true believers desire the sincere milk of the Word, and the desire of grace in this way is grace.

One said that the great saints in the calendar were, many of them, poor sinners. Mrs. Newton replied, they were poor saints indeed if they did not feel that they were great sinners.

The Lord has reasons, far beyond our knowing, for opening a wide door while He stops the mouth of a useful preacher. John Bunyan would not have done half the good he did, if he had remained preaching in Bedford instead of being shut up in Bedford prison.

Professors who own the doctrines of free grace often act inconsistently with their own principles when they are angry at the defects of others. A company of travelers fall into a pit, and one of them gets a passenger to draw him out. Now he should not be angry with the rest for falling in nor because they are not yet out as he is. He did not pull himself out. Therefore, instead of reproaching them, he should show them pity. He should avoid, at any rate, going down upon their ground again and show how much better and happier he is upon his own. We should take care that we do not make our profession of religion a receipt in full of all other obligations. A man truly illuminated will no more despise others than Bartimaeus, after his own eyes were opened would take a stick and beat every blind man he met.

It is pure mercy that refuses a particular request. A miser would pray very earnestly for gold, if he believed prayer would gain it. Whereas, if Christ had any favor to him He would take his gold away. A child walks in the garden in spring and sees cherries. He knows they are good fruit and therefore asks for them. "No, dear," says the father, "they are not yet ripe; stay until the season."

If I cannot take pleasure in infirmities, I can sometimes feel the profit of them. I can conceive a king to pardon a rebel and take him into his family, and then say, "I appoint you for a season to wear a fetter. At a certain season I will send a messenger to knock it off. In the meantime this fetter will serve to remind you of your state. It may humble you and restrain you from rambling."

I have read of many wicked popes, but the worst pope I ever met with is Pope Self.

The heir of a great estate, while a child, thinks more of a few shillings in his pocket than of his inheritance. So a Christian is often more elated by some frame of heart than by his title to glory.

I feel like a man who has no money in his pocket, but is allowed to draw for all he wants upon one infinitely rich. I am, therefore, at once both a beggar and a rich man.

Sometimes I compare the troubles which we have to undergo in the course of the year to a great bundle of fagots, far too large for us to lift. But God does not require us to carry the whole at once; He mercifully unties the bundle and gives us first one stick, which we are to carry today, and then another which we are to carry tomorrow, and so on. This we might easily manage if we would only take the burden appointed for us each day; but we chose to increase our troubles by carrying yesterday's stick over again today and adding tomorrow's burden to our load before we are required to bear it.

Endnote

1. The punctuation and a few terms have been changed in this chapter. Otherwise, Newton's sayings are left as originally written.

The church of St. Mary Woolnoth, built by Nicholas Hawksmoor in 1716–1721. Newton was appointed Rector in 1780. The church, surrounded by business and financial offices, has survived several efforts to demolish it.

The marble plaque with the words of Newton's epitah, which hangs above a side aisle of the church (photo by permission of St. Mary Woolnoth, London).

FOR FURTHER READING

Original sources:

Newton, John. *The Life and Spirituality of John Newton* (Vancouver: Regent College Publishing, 1998). Contains the text of Newton's *An Authentic Narrative of Some Remarkable Particulars in the Life of ********, and "Spiritual Letters on Growth in Grace," with an informative introduction by Bruce Hindmarsh.

Newton, John. *The Works of John Newton* (Edinburgh: Peter Brown, 1838. Republished by Banner of Truth, 1988).

Other works:

Davidson, Noel. *How Sweet the Sound: The Absorbing Story of John Newton and William Cowper* (Greenville, South Carolina: Emerald House, 1997).

Hindmarsh, Bruce. *John Newton and the English Evangelical Tradition* (Grand Rapids, Mich: Wm. B. Eerdmans Publishers, 2001).

Turner, Steve. *Amazing Grace: The Story of America's Most Beloved Song* (New York: HarperCollins Publishers, 2002).

For further information on the life of John Newton and William Cowper, visit the home page of the Cowper and Newton Museum at *www.mkheritage.co.uk/cnm*. Visitors to the Web site can take a virtual tour of Orchard Side, from 1768–86 the home of the poet and hymn-writer William Cowper and which now houses the Cowper and Newton Museum.

Amazing Grace:
366 Inspiring Hymn Stories for Daily Devotions

0-8254-3425-4

A national best-selling devotional book with more than 275,000 copies in print! Each of the 366 selections presents an inspiring, true-life experience behind the writing of a well-known hymn and the biblical truths drawn from it. Each day's selection includes a portion of the hymn, as well as suggested Scripture readings and meditations.